8 KEYS TO
END BULLYING

8 Keys to Mental Health Series

Babette Rothschild, Series Editor

The 8 Keys series of books provides consumers with brief, inexpensive, and high-quality self-help books on a variety of topics in mental health. Each volume is written by an expert in the field, someone who is capable of presenting evidence-based information in a concise and clear way. These books stand out by offering consumers cutting-edge, relevant theory in easily digestible portions, written in an accessible style. The tone is respectful of the reader and the messages are immediately applicable. Filled with exercises and practical strategies, these books empower readers to help themselves.

8 KEYS TO END BULLYING

STRATEGIES FOR PARENTS & SCHOOLS

────────

SIGNE WHITSON

FOREWORD BY BABETTE ROTHSCHILD

W. W. Norton & Company
New York • London

6/14

For information about permission to reproduce selections from this book, write to
Permissions, W. W. Norton & Company, Inc., 500 Fifth Avenue, New York, NY 10110

For information about special discounts for bulk purchases, please contact W. W.
Norton
Special Sales at specialsales@wwnorton.com or 800-233-4830

Manufacturing by Quad Graphics, Fairfield
Production manager: Leeann Graham

Library of Congress Cataloging-in-Publication Data

Whitson, Signe.
  8 keys to end bullying : strategies for parents & schools / Signe Whitson ; foreword by
Babette Rothschild. — First edition.
        pages cm.   (8 keys to mental health series)
Includes bibliographical references and index.
ISBN 978-0-393-70928-5 (pbk.)
  1. Bullying—Prevention.   2. Bullying in schools—Prevention.   3. Aggressiveness
in children.   I. Title.   II. Title: Eight keys to end bullying.
BF637.B85W48 2014
302.34'3—dc23
                                2014001241

ISBN: 978-0-393-70928-5 (pbk.)

W. W. Norton & Company, Inc., 500 Fifth Avenue, New York, N.Y. 10110
www.wwnorton.com
W. W. Norton & Company Ltd., Castle House, 75/76 Wells Street, London W1T 3QT

1 2 3 4 5 6 7 8 9 0

To Richard, Hannah, and Elise

and

to all of the awe-inspiring educators, counselors,
youth workers, and parents who know that
the little things are truly the big things
when it comes to making a difference
in the life of a child.

Contents

Foreword

Babette Rothschild, Series Editor

Bullying has always been a part of group and student dynamics. It used to be that all bullying was conducted in person (and behind the back). However, the invention of the computer, email, and the advent of online social networking has brought a whole other dimension to the problem. And, of course, it is not only children who are vulnerable to bullying. Adults can also be victimized, particularly (but not only) in the workplace.

Though it has not always been recognized as a serious, societal problem, in the last few decades bullying has increasingly gained the attention of the public eye, also in the media, as more and more violence is ascribed to victims of bullying: shootings, suicides, and the like. Psychologists and other mental health professionals and researchers have also jumped into the fray; the number of studies and research on bullying are growing as well.

A volume on bullying has always been at the top of the priority list for the 8 *Keys to Mental Health Series*. The question was, who should write it? Through her popular website, blog, and previous publications, Signe Whitson was an obvious candidate, at the forefront of the debate. She has long worked to combat bullying as both an author and educator and she tackles the problem with immense knowledge, experience, sensitivity, wit, and plenty of heart. There can be no doubt that she is on the side of the bullied and truly wants to see an end to victimization. At the same time she is full of common sense. She recognizes that if the definition of bullying becomes too broad and watered down, attention will be thinned and it risks being misdirected. So, first and foremost, she clearly distinguishes bullying from less serious sorts of unpleasant encounters such as rudeness and simple meanness. In doing so, she highlights the serious, and sometimes tragic, consequences of bullying. And she emphasizes just how common a problem it is.

Many of us can remember one or more incidents of bullying from our childhood as victim, participant, and/or observer. I can remember several, but one stands out in particular. One day in third grade a schoolmate asked me if I was a tomboy. I liked to climb trees, run, and play sports. And I'd heard that term used affectionately within my family for girls who liked such things. So I simply—and innocently—answered, "Yes." To be honest, I also hoped it would bond us as I'd seen her doing the same things and figured she was looking for a kindred spirit. However, within a day, "tomboy" became a swear word in the mouth of that schoolmate and anyone else she could bring on board. I was ostracized and called "tomboy" with derision at every opportunity.

What started as my innocent attempt at bonding turned into a nightmare for me. I don't remember how long it went on—days or weeks—but during that time "tomboys" weren't allowed at lunch tables, group games, etc. I don't believe that everyone participated, but enough so that my school life was made very difficult. I remember crying and begging to not have to go to school. My parents, though sympathetic, had no idea how to help me. Everyone knew what bullying was back then, but it was considered just a normal part of childhood. In 1958, no one recognized how bullying could crush a child's spirit.

Finally, my parents insisted that I fight back. I didn't really know what that meant, and they didn't know how to teach me, but I nonetheless became determined not to give in to the bullies. One day at recess as we were choosing our positions for a ball game, the schoolmate challenged me, "I don't want a tomboy in *my* field." Pulling myself together I replied, "Then leave!" Magically (and luckily) there was never a "tomboy" problem again. Of course, most bullies are not so easily deterred. I really do think I was lucky as I was on my own: no parent or teacher was there to intervene. And mine is not an example of the worst kind of bullying; I never so despaired that I considered suicide. Nonetheless, I can trace the effects of this incident into insecurities that I have had throughout my life in feeling comfortable participating in all sorts of groups.

8 Keys to End Bullying contains just what its title promises: concrete keys to identify the problem and end it. In an intimate, friendly reading style, Whitson gives specific, clear, helpful guidelines to parents, teachers and administrators, and community leaders on how to intervene in effective ways. Numerous news stories spotlight how much damage bullying can cause. Likewise, there are equally numerous inspiring examples of both small and big victories against bullying. Whitson includes examples of both. She also includes sample dialogue to follow for those who want to intervene to diffuse a difficult situation but don't know what to say—sentences you can actually use to talk with your child, your student, the parent of a bully, and so forth. Each chapter ends with "10 Practical Strategies" that can immediately be put into use.

Among many important points, Whitson highlights the central role of bystanders in both enabling and preventing bullying. I wish I had had the benefit of her guidance, myself, just a few years ago! I was shocked and dumbfounded to witness a respected psychiatrist bully and humiliate a workshop participant in front of the entire audience (120 or more professional therapists). You could have cut the air with a knife. I, myself, was frozen in place. Everyone else must have been as well because *no one* said or did *anything*. I am still haunted by my inability to respond, to stop the attack, or even to approach and offer support to the victim when she, some minutes later, left the room (and did not return). I still feel horrible about it. I think we were all intimidated by the arrogance and position of the speaker, and probably also afraid of professional backlash, or triggered by paralyzing memories of our own childhood victimization. I've promised myself that I'll never let that happen again, and luckily have not had the opportunity to test it. My experience further reminds me that getting anyone, also kids, to speak out against bullying is no easy matter. Even well-informed and otherwise usually assertive adults can also find themselves unable to act. However, now, thanks to Whitson's book, I feel that I am bolstered, supported, and well supplied with plenty of ammunition should another such situation arise.

Whitson's humanity and heartfelt investment in kids comes through on every page. She gives us hope that bullying does not need to be tolerated. And that it can be better than managed, it can be stopped.

Introduction

Erin had her first heartbreak at the tender age of 8. During the first week of second grade, she met a little girl named Kristy and, as so charmingly happens at that age, the two became best friends within an instant. The girls bonded over their love of a made-for-television pop group and could be spotted breaking out in spontaneous song and dance together whenever an unstructured school moment was offered. They quickly became a package deal inside and outside of the classroom, arranging lunch dates at school and playdates when school was not in session.

For a few weeks, all Erin's mother heard was "Kristy says this" and "Kristy likes that" and "Kristy told me I had to do such and such." Erin's mom admitted that she was a bit swept up in Kristy fever as well, enjoying how much pleasure her young daughter was taking from the friendship. Until it all ended.

Just as the warm days of early September turned to the brisk chill of late October, Erin began to experience the cold harshness of relational aggression, a confusing and painful form of bullying that I define in Key 1. In Erin's world, relational aggression felt like a breakup—or more like getting dumped. The first incident her mom noticed was Kristy shoving Erin off a chair during the school's open house night—not in a game of musical chairs. (Erin's mom checked.) Not because Kristy was angry at Erin and lost her temper, as many young school-age children do. (Kristy was a very measured, even-tempered girl with good control over her emotions.) By all later accounts, Kristy pushed Erin simply because she wanted to—she was making a deliberate choice to assert power and to be cruel.

Heart in her throat and mama-bear claws ready to scratch, Erin's mother watched as the girls' teacher walked over to the scene of the shoving. The teacher asked, "Erin, are you all right? Did Kristy hurt you?" Even at the tender age of 8, however, Erin knew she could not risk angering Kristy by identifying her act as unwanted. By second grade, the young girl had already adopted the belief that she had no choice but to say, "No, it's okay." Kristy quickly followed up by adding, "We were just playing," with a glib smile that seemed to satisfy the teacher, especially amid the array of open house activities. Erin became even more confused. "Is Kristy my friend or not?" she remembers wondering. She decided to go with the former conclusion and, with that hope springing eternal, plunged in for more "friendship" the next day.

That next day, and in the coming weeks, Kristy kept the sugarcoated hostility and the under-the-radar aggression going. At the lunch table, she quietly admonished Erin that she couldn't sit with the girls because she had a "boy's name." Sting. When picking partners for a game in the gym, she loudly instructed everyone not to pick Erin because she was "the worst runner of all." Burn. When Erin asked her for a playdate after school, Kristy told her flat out, "You're not my best friend anymore." Puncture.

Erin suffered most of these wounds in dutiful silence, though her mother did notice that all of her daughter's enthusiasm for school had vanished and her normally joyful social demeanor had become very cautious. The afternoon after the "not my best friend anymore" proclamation, Erin's mom heard her daughter crying in her bedroom. She asked Erin what was wrong and Erin asked her in return, "Mama, how can I change to make Kristy like me again?"

This event occurred years ago, though Erin's mom still gets tears in her eyes when she recalls the pain and self-doubt her young child endured. For anyone who says the problems of kids are insignificant, I assure you that the pain caused by bullying at any age is soul crushing.

*   *   *

As a licensed social worker and professional educator on issues related to child and adolescent emotional and behavioral health, I get to do quite a bit of traveling, training, writing, talking, and (most important!) listening. In all of these forms of contact, it is you—professionals and parents concerned about bullying—that I enjoy interacting with the most because bullying is the subject matter that stirs the deepest emotions and elicits the most impassioned responses. From professionals' triumphant accounts of successful efforts to halt bullying in their schools to parents' heart-wrenching stories of their kids' unending torment by cruel peers, the truth is that everyone has a story when it comes to bullying.

Some days, I cry right along with the story sharers as they retell their experiences. Other days, I cheer for the champions of children who never take "no" for an answer when it comes to stepping in to stop bullying. Most days, I cringe at how ubiquitous cruelty has become; the bullying that happens to young people truly stays with young people—sometimes for the rest of their lives—whether it originates in person, on the Internet, at home, in school, or anywhere in between.

So why do I look forward to speaking and writing about a topic that is so fraught with unkind actions and lasting pain? The truth is that aside from the tears and the hurt, I feel something even more powerful; I feel hope.

I believe we have an opportunity to change the culture of bullying among young people and I think it begins with the powerful actions of the people who live and work with kids every day. There are no one-step answers to a problem this widespread and I won't give pat strategies or formulaic answers to minimize the work that lies ahead of all of us. Yet I know from experience that real change happens person to person and I am hopeful every time I reach out to a group of professionals and parents that change can begin with us.

By the very act of picking up this book, you have shown that you are interested in strategies to make kids' lives better. That's what 8 *Keys to End Bullying* is all about. This is a book about hope. Not wing-and-a-prayer-type hope, but rather the knowledge that consistent, everyday acts by attuned, nurturing adults can make conditions better for kids. This book provides educators, mental health professionals, parents, and youth workers with jargon-free, easy-to-implement prevention and intervention strategies for changing the culture of unwanted aggression among kids, tweens, and teens.

How to Use This Book

The information in 8 *Keys to End Bullying* is designed with an activist reader in mind. Without theory, there is no practice, so each chapter features current research and up-to-date information on bullying that readers can use to deepen their knowledge of the dynamics of unwanted aggression among young people. On the other hand, most professionals and parents I know turn to books when they want an answer to the question, "What do I do?" Each key in this book provides practical, how-to guidance for how to manage specific aspects of bullying.

I am the type of person who likes to read nonfiction books with a pen in my hand. I underline, I take notes, and I dog-ear pages with abandon. When I know that a piece of information or suggested strategy would work for me, I want to be able to refer back to it over and over again. I have written this book with that goal in mind for you—that from your reading, you will think new thoughts, be inspired by new ideas, and want to try them out again and again. I hope you will jot down your thoughts as you read this book.

Speaking of writing, each key features several exercises designed to challenge you to apply what you are reading to your own life—either your experiences growing up or incidents of bullying in your world today. The exercises will be most meaningful if you take some time, as you are reading, to write down answers. Several of the exercises call for you to put pen to paper and commit to specific actions with kids. Others ask you to reflect on how you can make the biggest impact in the life of a vulnerable child. I hope you will do both, as this extra time spent processing the book can help turn words into actions and actions into positive changes for young people.

Correspondence and Feedback

This book is made rich by the real-life anecdotes you will read in each of the keys. Many are from my own work, while others come from the lives of the professionals and parents I meet though my training sessions, who have generously shared with me their stories—and, more profoundly, their children's stories. I learn and grow professionally every time I listen to others' accounts of bullying. If you have an experience related to bullying that you would like to share, I welcome you to send it to me. Please know that I may not be able to respond directly to every e-mail and that I prefer not to give advice about particular situations without the benefit of full contextual knowledge, but I will appreciate your taking the time to tell your story. I also invite you to send your feedback on the usefulness and practicality of the information and strategies provided in this book. Please direct all correspondence and feedback via my Web site (www.signewhitson.com) or through e-mail (signe@signewhitson.com).

8 KEYS TO
END BULLYING

KNOW BULLYING WHEN YOU SEE BULLYING

The Who, What, When, Why, and How of Unwanted Aggression

What is bullying?

This three-word question seems like an obvious enough place to begin a book about bringing an end to bullying. The colloquial answer to it, however, may be as varied as the personal stories that professionals, parents, and children have to share about their experiences with unwanted aggression. I celebrate that kids who are bullied now have a voice. It was not long ago that the "kids will be kids" mentality prevailed and young people were denigrated as "weak" or as "tattletales" for reaching out to adults for help in coping with relentless cruelty in their schools and communities.

I have been moved to tears on too many occasions while listening to parents share their feelings of outrage and helplessness over their kids' experiences with bullying in school. I can't get out of my head one searingly painful account of humiliation in a high school cafeteria that a young girl recently shared with me, as she walked from table to table, meeting rejection after rejection from an organized group of classmates who had prearranged not to let her have a seat at lunch—ever. I am haunted by stories of relentless physical and verbal bullying on school buses, in locker rooms, at recess, and online. It never gets old for me; I am routinely astounded by every new account; the merciless cruelty makes my jaw drop every time.

It is important for me to begin this book by establishing that without doubt, many of the stories of bullying that are shared with me are horrifying and some are unspeakably vicious. But now, I also want to be honest and share that some of the stories are . . . well . . . really not so bad.

Take this story recently shared with me by a neighbor who had just learned of my professional work:

"Signe, I saw your picture in the paper last week. Congratulations! I didn't know you worked with bullied students. It's so important that you do—things have gotten so bad! Last week, my daughter was bullied really badly after school! She was getting off of her bus when this kid from our neighborhood threw a fistfull of leaves right in her face! When she got home, she still had leaves in the hood of her coat. It's just awful! I just don't know what to do about these bullies."

"Was she very upset when she got home?" I empathized.

"No. She just brushed the leaves off and told me they were having fun together," she said.

"Oh," I answered knowingly, aware that oftentimes kids try to downplay victimization by bullies, due to the embarrassment and shame they feel. "Did you get the sense she was covering for the boy?" I asked.

"No, no. She really seemed to think it was fun. She said that she threw leaves back at him, which I told her never to do again! The nerve of those kids."

"Those kids," I clarified. "Was it just the one boy throwing leaves or were there a bunch of kids all ganging up on her?"

"No, it was just this one boy that lives about a block from us," she assured me.

"Is he usually mean to her? Has he bothered her after school before?" I asked, eager at this point to figure out what the bullying issue was.

"No. I don't think so at least. That was the first time she

ever said anything about him. It was definitely the first time that I noticed the leaves all over her coat. But it better be the last time! I won't stand for her being bullied by that kid. Next time, I am going to make sure the principal knows what is going on after school lets out!"

While I always want to be careful not to minimize anyone's experience and a part of me suspects that the sharing of this particular story may simply have been this parent's spontaneous way of making conversation with me in a store aisle, I hear these "alarming" (read: benign) stories often enough to conclude that there is a real need to draw a distinction between behavior that is rude, behavior that is mean, and behavior that is characteristic of bullying. Bestselling children's author Trudy Ludwig (2013) distinguishes the following terms.

- Rude = inadvertently saying or doing something that hurts someone else.

A particular relative of mine (whose name it would be rude of me to mention) often looks my curly red hair up and down before inquiring in a sweet tone, "Have you ever thought about coloring your hair?" or "I think you look so sophisticated when you straighten your hair, Signe." This doting family member thinks she is helping me. The rest of the people in the room cringe at her boldness and I am left to wonder if being a brunette would suit me. Her comments can sting, but remembering that they come from a place of love—in her mind—helps me to remember what to do with the advice.

From kids, rude behavior might look more like laughing when an opponent strikes out, pointing out that a classmate is wearing the same shirt twice in one week, jumping ahead in a line, or even throwing a crushed-up pile of leaves in someone's face. On their own, any of these behaviors could appear to be elements of bullying, but when looked at in context, incidents of rudeness are usually spontaneous, unplanned inconsideration, based on thoughtlessness, poor manners, or narcissism, but not meant to actually hurt someone.

- Mean = purposefully saying or doing something to hurt someone once (or maybe twice).

The main distinction between rude and mean behavior has to do with intention; while rudeness is often unintentional, mean behavior very much aims to hurt or depreciate someone. Kids are mean to each other when they criticize clothing, appearance, intelligence, coolness, or just about anything else they can find to put down. Meanness also sounds like words spoken in anger—impulsive cruelty that is often regretted in short order. Commonly, meanness in kids sounds an awful lot like this:

"Are you seriously considering trying out for basketball? You suck at sports! Why don't you just go back to your video games, loser?"
"You are so fat/ugly/stupid/gay."
"I hate you!"

Make no mistake; mean behaviors can wound deeply and adults can make a huge difference in the lives of young people when they hold kids accountable for being mean. Yet meanness is different from bullying in important ways that should be understood and differentiated when it comes to intervention.

- Bullying = intentionally aggressive behavior, repeated over time, that involves an imbalance of power.

Daniel Olweus (Olweus et al., 2007), founder of the internationally recognized Olweus Bullying Prevention Program, defines bullying as having three key elements: an intent to harm, a power imbalance, and repeated acts or threats of unwanted aggressive behavior. Kids who bully can be relentless, acting out against others with no sense of regret, remorse, or mercy.

Olweus also draws a useful distinction between rough play, real fighting, and bullying.

- **Rough play:** In rough play, kids are usually friends and enjoy a relatively equal balance of power. There is no intent to harm and the mood is friendly, positive, and mutual. Kids who are wrestling over command of a stray ball or throwing elbows in an effort to capture the title of King of the Hill are happily engaged in rough play—though sometimes much to the chagrin of adult onlookers. This would also be the best way to characterize the leaf-throwing example described above.

- **Real fighting:** In real fighting, kids are usually not friends but there is a relatively equal balance of power. Like meanness, this behavior is usually spontaneous and not repeated. There is intent to harm and the mood is negative, aggressive, and tense. When a brawl breaks out on a practice field after a particularly competitive game, opponents are engaging in real fighting. When two teens come to blows one day after school over a shared love interest, they are fighting.

- **Bullying:** Bullying is distinct from rough play and real fighting in that the kids involved are usually not friends and there is an unequal balance of power. There is an intent to harm and the mood differs for the aggressor and the victim. When one person organizes all of her friends to jump a classmate after school, because she believes the targeted peer has stolen her love interest, then follows it up by sending embarrassing photos of the girl via text to their entire grade, the incident has moved deep into the realm of bullying.

As we will see in greater detail in the next section, incidents of bullying may be physical, verbal, relational, and/or carried out via technology. Before we move on, however, we return to the fundamental question of why it is important to accurately define bullying and to distinguish it from other forms of aggression.

In our culture of 24-7 news cycles and social media sound bites, we have a better opportunity than ever before to bring attention to important issues. In the last few years, adults have collectively paid attention to the issue of bullying like never before; millions of school children have been given a voice; 49 states in the United States have passed antibullying legislation, and thousands of adults have been trained in important strategies to keep kids safe and dignified in schools and communities. These are significant achievements.

At the same time, however, gratuitous references to bullying have bred cynicism in some and caused others to think the little boy is crying wolf. When people improperly classify rudeness and mean behavior as bullying—whether to simply make conversation or to bring attention to their short-term discomfort—we are all put at risk of becoming numb to the true seriousness of the term and tuning out when truly troubled kids need adult intervention. What's more, as *Sticks and Stones* author Emily Bazelon (2013) points out, the overdiagnosis of bullying diverts precious fiscal and human resources away from kids who need them most.

It is important to distinguish between rudeness, meanness, and bullying so that teachers, school administrators, counselors, police, youth workers, parents, and kids all know what to pay attention to and when to intervene. The bottom line is that rates of school bullying drop significantly when adults share a common understanding of what bullying is (and what it is not) and agree to intervene consistently whenever they become aware that it is happening (Wright, 2013). Bullying is a pervasive issue among young people, but it is also a manageable one when we refuse to allow false alarms to overwhelm us. As we have heard too often in the news, a child's well-being depends on a nonjaded adult's ability to discern between rudeness at the bus stop and life-altering bullying.

How Do Kids Bully?

PACER's National Bullying Prevention Center (2012) reports that nearly one-third of all school-aged children are bullied each year—upward of 13 million students. Even taking into account that rude and mean behavior is sometimes mislabeled as bullying, this phenomenon is still clearly a widespread issue among school-aged youth. The ability to recognize bullying in all of its forms is essen-

Exercise: Helping Kids Understand the Differences Between Rudeness, Meanness, and Bullying

Just as adults need to understand and acknowledge the differences between rude, mean, and bullying behaviors, young people benefit when they can distinguish between these categories. Talk to kids about each behavior, being careful to draw out the distinct characteristics of each one at a level appropriate for their age group. If you are working with kids in a school or community setting, assign small groups of kids (three to five kids per group) to develop three written scenarios—one that represents rudeness, one that represents meanness, and one that represents bullying.

Challenge group members to carefully think through how each scenario differs from the others. If time allows, it can be most impactful to encourage kids to act out their scenarios as mini skits for the large group. Facilitate discussion after each skit about what behaviors were demonstrated and why they are characteristic of rudeness, meanness, or bullying. Encourage discussion about how most behaviors occur on a continuum and explore how rudeness can become meanness, which can become bullying over time.

Ask kids for their thoughts on why it's important to make a distinction between the behaviors. Encourage them to talk about occasions in which they mistook a mean comment for bullying or excused actual bullying as simple rudeness.

This exercise works equally well for professionals as an in-service training activity and with parents during group or even one-on-one meetings.

tial to early intervention and bringing an end to unwanted aggression. Bullying occurs in four basic ways:

1. **Physical aggression**

   Acts of violence were once the gold standard of bullying—the proverbial sticks and stones that made adults in charge stand up and take notice. This kind of bullying includes hitting, punching, pinching, kicking, spitting, tripping, hair-pulling, slamming a child into a locker, taking or breaking someone's possessions, and a range of other behaviors that involve outward physical aggression.

2. **Verbal aggression**

   Spoken taunting, teasing, name calling, sexual comments, and threats are the kind of verbal aggression that the parents of most readers advised their kids to just ignore. We now know that despite the old adage, words can, indeed, hurt us and can even cause profound, lasting harm. As we will see in Key 5, advising young people to ignore verbal bullying is now considered some of the least effective advice around.

3. **Relational aggression**

   Relational aggression is a form of bullying in which kids use their friendship—or the threat of taking their friendship away—to hurt someone. Social exclusion, shunning, hazing, and rumor spreading are all forms of this pervasive type of bullying that can be especially beguiling and crushing to kids.

4. **Cyberbullying**

   Cyberbullying is a specific form of bullying that involves technology. According to Hinduja and Patchin (2010) of the Cyberbullying Research Center, it is the "willful and repeated harm inflicted through the use of computers, cell phones, and other electronic devices." Notably, the likelihood of repeated harm is especially high with cyberbullying because electronic messages can be accessed by multiple parties, resulting in repeated exposure and repeated harm.

Exercise: Recognizing Bullying in All of Its Forms

Bullying cannot be pinned down to a singular behavior or form. Rather, most kids who bully use multiple tactics to inflict repetitive acts of unwanted aggression on their weaker victims. It is helpful for adults and kids to be knowledgeable about the varied ways in which bullying is acted out and the specific behaviors that are used.

Before moving on to the next section, make a list of the ways in which you have seen bullying played out. Use the four categories listed above (physical aggression, verbal aggression, relational aggression, and cyberbullying) to organize your list. Challenge yourself to write down at least five specific examples for each category—truly, the list is almost endless.

Next, think about which behaviors on the list occur most commonly in your setting or among the kids that you know. Put a star next to these behaviors. These high-frequency behaviors merit your extra attention and responsiveness. Moreover, these are the key behaviors that you can educate kids about, teaching them specific strategies for recognizing and responding effectively to this type of aggression.

Also consider:

- Are there specific bullying behaviors on your list that occur less frequently but inflict more physical or emotional pain?
- Which behaviors on the list are kids most likely to report?
- Which behaviors cause more confusion or humiliation to young people and are therefore less likely to be shared with adults?
- Physical and verbal aggression tend to be easier to observe than relational and online aggression. What can you do to make sure that you are aware of and prepared to intervene in all forms of bullying?
- What will you do to respond to the behaviors on your list, when you become aware that they are occurring?

Who Bullies?

When I was a young child, I recall hearing stories about bullies who would hide out behind the bushes along a child's walk to school, waiting to snatch lunch money. Although I packed my lunch every single day, I still worried that these lurking "big boys" might try to take my milk money. I was vigilant for five years straight! Thankfully, those thug-type bullies never came for me, but to this day I remember vividly the bully prototype I feared for so many years.

In reality, bullies come in all genders and ages, shapes and sizes. They come from troubled families and nurturing ones, wealthy backgrounds and those of low socioeconomic status. They can lurk like bad guys, but just as often, they hide in plain sight as a child's best friend. The reality is that almost any child can bully another child on any given day. To be clear: There is no singular answer to the question of who bullies, no precise profile for educators to review at the beginning of a school year, and no systematic checklist that concerned parents can use to guide their sons and daughters in making healthy friendship choices.

Rather, as best-selling children's author Trudy Ludwig (2010) writes in her book, *Confessions of a Former Bully,* all different types of kids wear bully hats on certain occasions. Committee for Children research scientist Brian Smith (2013) explains that "it's more accurate to think of bullying as a social behavior or process than as something that one person does, much less something that one person is. We know from research that bullying happens because of a range of influences that are almost all beyond any given individual."

When we, as adults, understand that by their very nature, kids are works in progress, and that their behavior on any given day—or even on repeated occasions—is subject to guidance and improvement, we stop placing them in harmful categories such as "bully," "troublemaker," and "problem child" and begin to view them as young people who deserve to be taught better ways to behave. Allison Wedell Schumacher (2013) writes that using the word "bully" as a noun suggests that the young person may never break out of that role, whereas describing the behavior as a verb acknowledges the hopeful truth that the child is capable of stopping the aggression, casting aside the bully hat, and making better choices.

Exercise: What Does Your Bullying Hat Look Like?

Before moving on, take a brief moment to recall a day in your life on which you behaved badly toward someone else. It could be a recent occasion when you lashed out at a peer due to anger or a time from your childhood when you ganged up on a friend. Each of us has a moment (or two) that we regret.

Hopefully, we all have been able to make amends and be forgiven for our mistakes. Assume your actions were not excused, however. Imagine how you might feel if you were forever judged by others based on your most embarrassing, shameful, uncharacteristic moment. What would people say about you? How might they treat you differently in the long term? How could their lingering judgments impact the way you think about yourself?

This reflective exercise is a good way to get in touch with how easy it is to behave badly on occasion and how devastating it would be for a young person to be judged, labeled, and pigeonholed for a single day's worth of regrettable behavior. This activity is also a good springboard for discussion among adults on how we go about using an incident of bullying behavior not as an occasion for rote punishment and long-term grudges but rather as an opportunity to teach new skills, develop stronger relationships, and make better choices.

Can Siblings Truly Bully Each Other?

For some siblings, squabbling comes as naturally as breathing. Bickering over the remote control and competing for the bigger, better bedroom have long been considered a normal part of family life. Indeed, many experts contend that brothers and sisters stand to gain from conflict, as the working through of disagreements nets them valuable skills in conflict resolution, problem solving, and self-control. While there is arguably an upside to some familial anger, a study by Corinna Jenkins Tucker (Tucker, Finkelhor, Turner, & Shattuck, 2013) finds that when sibling rivalry crosses the line into bullying, kids experience psychological effects that are as damaging as the distress caused by peers at school or on the playground. The criteria that mark the divide between normal bickering and destructive bullying are the same within families as they are outside of them: Parents and caretakers should be on alert whenever they see signs of repetitive cruelty, intent to harm, and an imbalance of power in sibling dynamics. Efforts to end bullying begin at home. Decisive intervention by parents has the doubly positive potential of protecting targeted young people from abusive behavior and teaching aggressive children that this kind of behavior is unacceptable in the home, at school, and anywhere in their lives.

Why Do Kids Bully?

In this section, we move beyond the damning question of who bullies to explore the more solution-focused subject of why kids bully. As adults put their efforts into understanding what drives kids to bully, we gain important insights that lead us to effective interventions for bringing an end to this destructive behavior. While the precise, minute-to-minute motivations for bullying are as varied as the kids themselves, there are four main explanations we can look to.

To Gain Social Status

As a child, when I would be teased by my peers about my fiery red hair or my face full of freckles, I remember my mom assuring me "they are just jealous" or "they are suffering from low self-esteem." Now, my mama was right about many, many things, but a part of me always believed that she was missing the mark when it came to the motivations of my classmates.

In fact, the myth that the bully has low self-esteem has largely been debunked in recent years. Antibullying expert Dr. Joel Haber (2007) points out that many kids who bully are actually quite popular, smart, confident, and socially adept. What researchers are now finding out is that many kids who bully are not driven by insecurity but rather are motivated by the desire to increase their own social status.

A groundbreaking study by University of California, Davis sociology professors Robert Faris and Diane Felmlee (2011) reveals that the drive to gain social status has everything to do with why many kids use aggression toward one another. Further, Faris and Felmlee identify harassment, rumor spreading, and exclusion (the hallmarks of verbal and relational aggression) as the most effective tactics of kids who cast aside friendships for a chance at popularity.

To Maintain Power and Control

Kids who bully tend to enjoy the sense of power and control they get from dominating interactions and manipulating others. One of the most common ways bullying plays out in schools is through the "mean girl" dynamic, in which an alpha female, or queen bee, exerts power and influence over who is in and who is out of the peer group. Her friends (read: followers) live in fear that she will turn on them next if they don't do as she says. Take this actual example from an urban middle school:

Zoe and Taylor had been friends since elementary school. When things were good, they had a lot of fun together. Taylor explained to me once that Zoe was "always around to hang out after school" and invited her over a lot. She also confided that Zoe criticized her a lot and made her feel badly about her clothing, her taste in music, and her other friends. Before I could open my mouth to ask why Taylor continued this friendship, she explained, "If I tell her how I feel, she'll turn everyone else against me."

On a Monday in the school lunch cafeteria, Zoe told their classmate Kylie that she couldn't sit at their table. When Taylor moved over to make room for Kylie, Zoe warned her, "If you're friends with her, you can't be friends with me." Taylor quickly put her lunch tray back and mouthed to Kylie, "Sorry—maybe tomorrow."

That afternoon, Taylor found Kylie after school and apologized for what had happened at lunch. She asked Kylie to sit with her on the bus ride home.

Within the hour, Taylor received this text from Zoe: "You are a slut and a bitch. Everyone hates you. Do not come to my party this weekend." Taylor tried all night to text, call, and message Zoe to ask what she was so angry about, but Zoe never responded to her.

The next day in school, none of the kids in her homeroom would make eye contact with Taylor. At lunch, there was no space at her normal table. In her seat sat Kylie, right next to Zoe, laughing, giggling, and hovering over a cell phone. When she approached the table, the laughter stopped, followed by deafening silence. The deep freeze from her peers that Taylor had spent so much time fearing had come true and even Kylie, the friend Taylor risked ostracism for, had turned her back as well. Zoe turned around, smirked at Taylor, and announced, "Sorry—maybe tomorrow."

Dynamics of power and control are wielded through physical aggression and intimidation as well. In an urban high school, a 15-year-old freshman, Jeremy, was of small physical stature but big bravado. He often claimed to "rule the school" and bragged about how he kept others in line. While the adults in the school joked about Jeremy's Napoleon complex, to most students, he was no laughing matter. One afternoon, Jeremy was brought to the school office after punching a classmate in the stomach during their technology class. When questioned about the circumstances,

Jeremy explained calmly, "I told Ben that I wanted to use the computer in the first row. That's my computer. He sat there anyway. I even warned him a second time to move. Usually, I don't give second warnings, but today, I was being a nice guy. He deserved what he got. In fact, I went easy on him for what he did. I don't even know why I am in here. He's the one you should be talking to. He stole my computer."

Kids like Zoe and Jeremy, who bully in order to maintain power and control over their peers, often share in common a lack of empathy. For some, deficits in empathy appear in the young person's behavior across the board. For others, it is the intense but situational drive for social status, power, and control that causes them to disregard the rights, needs, and feelings of others. In either case, the development of empathy is a critical intervention strategy for adults working with kids who bully in this way, which is covered in Key 5.

To Enjoy Peer Attention

For young people who value social status, power, and control, it is through the attention of their peer group that they gain these perceived rewards. Anytime that bystanders laugh, encourage, go along with, or even stay silent in fear of bullying behaviors, the aggressor is socially reinforced and becomes more likely to continue this behavior in the future. An important key, then, in bringing an end to bullying is to understand the role of bystander behavior and to change it in such a way as to stop the social reinforcement that peers provide to kids who bully (see Key 6).

An explanation for why young people are so motivated by the attention of their peers can be found in neuroscience. A 2008 study by Temple University psychologist Laurence Steinberg demonstrates that the ventral striatum, an important structure in the brain's reward circuitry, is more active in teens when they are in the presence of their friends than when they are alone. In applying these findings to the science of bullying, Steinberg explains, "To the extent teenagers think bullying will elevate their status in the eyes of their peers—the immediate reward—they may not be paying as much attention to the longer-term cost" (as cited in Bazelon, 2013, p. 47). The "longer-term cost" has to do with behavioral consequences for the child who bullies but also with the lasting impact that bullying has on its victims. When kids' brains are hijacked by the intense rewards of peer attention, otherwise empathic kids can temporarily be caught up in a moment and lose touch with their compassion for others. Knowing this, adults can play a preemptive role in teaching kids to slow down their actions, think about what they are doing, and make conscious regard for others a priority in all of their peer interactions (see Key 5).

Because They Can

Thus far in examining the powerful motivations that drive kids to bully, we have concentrated on social factors. Now, we turn to something much simpler: opportunity.

Most bullying occurs in places where there is limited to no adult supervision. In school, the majority of unwanted aggression occurs in locations like the lunchroom, the locker room, the playground, the bathroom, the hallways, the bus, and online where adults are typically not present. In Key 3, we will look specifically at practical ways that the strategically increased presence of adults can significantly decrease the opportunity for bullying behavior by young people.

The second, and perhaps more disturbing, side of opportunity involves not the absence of adults, but rather the abdication of responsibility by adults who dismiss bullying as a rite of passage or disavow responsibility, saying, "It's not in my job description." According to the Center for Safe Schools (2012), adult attitudes toward bullying profoundly affect a young person's perception of the behavior. When adults indicate to young people—through their words, actions, or inactions—that bullying will be tolerated, young people may mistakenly intuit that the behavior is a normal and acceptable part of their world. For kids who are motivated by social status, power, control, and peer attention, adult indifference becomes a guilt-free ticket to ride.

In the last section of this chapter, as we examine the question of whose responsibility it is to stop bullying, we address the role that responsible adults play in lessening the opportunity for kids to bully by taking a stand to prioritize kids' dignity and safety.

Who Is Bullied?

Much as we cannot paint all kids who bully with the same brush, there is no single profile that pinpoints kids who will be victimized by their peers. Yet there are clearly identifiable elements that many bullied kids have in common. In this section, we look at six distinct characteristics and qualities of kids who are particularly vulnerable to bullying.

Kids With Disabilities

According to the U.S. Department of Health and Human Services, young people with physical, developmental, intellectual, emotional, and sensory disabilities are more likely to be bullied than their peers. Bearing in mind that bullying involves an imbalance of power, kids with disabilities are often considered to be an easy mark for unwanted aggression because of their relative physical vulnerability, academic challenges, and social skill struggles. One mother recently shared with me how vulnerable her 4-year-old son was among his preschool-aged peers:

> Nate struggled with selective mutism, a consistent failure to speak in specific social situations, despite speaking in others. Like other children with selective mutism, Nate understood language, but due to an underlying anxiety condition, did not speak outside of his home or to anyone but close family members. One day, at school pickup, as his mother approached the door to Nate's classroom, she could see through

a glass window that two young classmates were repeatedly hitting Nate on the forehead with their open palms. The classroom teacher was nowhere to be seen. For more than a minute, the mother stood knocking helplessly at the locked door, unable to get in, watching the scene continue. Nate, unable to speak to tell the kids to stop or to get the teacher's attention, was trapped in place by his peers.

Today, fully recovered from his disorder, Nate is able to talk openly about his feelings of powerlessness at the unchecked aggression. He tells his mother it was not a one-time occurrence, but rather a pattern of behavior that happened with regularity at his school. He recalls his peers demanding that he speak to them and, when he could not do so, they would hit him in their attempts to force the issue. Unable to speak to explain his own silence, Nate was a sitting duck for the unwanted aggression of his classmates.

James Wendorf (2012) of the National Center for Learning Disabilities calls bullying a pandemic for children with disabilities, citing that 60% of students with special needs are bullied each day, compared with 25% of all students. The U.S. Department of Health and Human Services (2013) identifies several groups of young people who are at a particularly high risk for being bullied, including kids with:

- Attention-deficit and attention-deficit/hyperactivity disorder (ADHD).
- Severe allergies. These kids face a range of ridicule, from being teased about their allergies to being purposefully exposed to life-threatening allergens.
- Physical disabilities that impact appearance, abilities, and movement, including cerebral palsy, muscular dystrophy, hemiplegia, epilepsy, and spina bifida.
- Insulin-dependent diabetes.
- A speech impediment or stuttering disorder.

- Anxiety disorders.
- Learning disabilities.
- Autism spectrum disorder (ASD).

According to the Centers for Disease Control and Prevention (2012), approximately 1 in every 88 children is identified with ASD, making it one of the most prevalent disorders among young people. Moreover, it is estimated that children with ASD are bullied at three times the rate of kids not identified as being on the spectrum, making it an important focus area for any adult interested in bringing an end to bullying.

Autism, by its very nature, is a social disability; kids with ASD often miss social cues and respond inappropriately (or not at all) to others. This social awkwardness and diminished ability to understand the complicated and ever-changing social hierarchies of their peer groups make them especially vulnerable to kids who bully. What's more, because of their difficulties making and keeping friends, kids with ASD often tend to be socially isolated—another risk factor for victimization that we examine shortly.

Kids Who Are Overweight or Obese

Obesity is also a major factor that makes children vulnerable to being bullied. According to a University of Michigan study published in *Pediatrics* (Lumeng et al., 2010), obese children are more likely to be bullied than their peers regardless of sex, race, socioeconomic status, social skills, or academic achievement. Researchers found that an obese child's odds of being bullied were a whopping 63% higher than those of a healthy-weight peer.

The lead investigator, Dr. Julie C. Lumeng, believes the high rate of bullying reflects a general societal prejudice against obese people that young children pick up on. Because there is a widespread view that obesity is all about a lack of self-control and laziness, kids come to view obesity as a character flaw, rather than as a physical trait, and therefore rationalize that it is okay to tease an overweight peer. Indeed, the stigmatization of obesity seems to be the last acceptable prejudice in our society and obese children feel the sting of unabashed disdain from their peers.

LGBT Youth

Lesbian, gay, bisexual, and transgender (LGBT) youth experience bullying at exceptionally high rates compared to their heterosexual peers. Dan Savage (2012), author of *It Gets Better: Coming Out, Overcoming Bullying, and Creating a Life Worth Living*, states that nine out of ten LGBT youths report being bullied in school. In recent years, the media has paid special attention to the suicides of several LGBT youths, including Rutgers freshman Tyler Clementi and 14-year-old Jamey Rodemeyer. While most experts agree that bullying is rarely the sole factor in a youth's decision to end his or her life, LGBT teens are four to seven times more likely to attempt suicide than their peers. This extreme rate of victimization and self-inflicted violence among LGBT populations screams for schools and communities to reach out to LGBT youth in more effective ways. I'll talk about specific ways that adults can go beyond teaching tolerance and start fostering cultures of acceptance in Key 3.

Kids Who Are Socially Isolated

Young people who lack a network of friends to back them up or who are afraid of reaching out to others become ideal targets for bullies. Bullying, in fact, is all about creating social isolation. A bully's main strategy is to make a victim feel alone and powerless, whether it be through the use of physical intimidation, verbal taunting, withdrawing friendship, rallying others to reject, ignore, and ostracize a peer, or using technology to spread rumors and ruin reputations.

Kids with disabilities, kids who are overweight or obese, and LGBT youth often find themselves socially isolated—either because their differences make them less able to establish friendships or because their peers fear becoming socially ostracized if they associate with bullied youth. A preexisting vulnerability to being bullied coupled with a lack of social support becomes a double whammy for the young person, digging him into a hole that he doesn't have the social skills or social capital to get out of. Harnessing the power of peer support for socially isolated kids is key in helping those victimized by bullying (see Key 6).

Kids Who Crave Popularity

So far in this section, we have talked about vulnerable populations of young people who too often exist at the bottom of their school's social ladder and therefore become easy marks for kids who bully. This is the more heartless and cowardly end of bullying behavior—picking on the underdog. As the Faris and Felmlee (2011) study points out, however, a significant portion of the bullying that occurs in schools and peer groups has to do with status rivalries among relative equals.

Kids who crave popularity may actually contribute to their own vulnerability to bullying when they use aggression as a tool of social climbing. Think of it as a game of social whack-a-mole; by putting down a peer, a young person experiences a temporary rise in status, only to become immediately vulnerable to being whacked by the next peer who is playing the same childish game. While some may call this instant karma, it is certain that there are no winners in this game of repeated social aggression.

Kids Who Are Volatile: The Bully-Victim

"Bully-victim" is a term used by some to describe young people who both show aggression toward their peers and tend to be frequent targets of aggressive behavior. Kids who are identified as bully-victims often struggle to regulate their emotional responses; they can be volatile and tend to be easily overwhelmed by their feelings. When compared to kids who bully for any of the other reasons cited in this section, bully-victims are more anxious, depressed, lonely, and high strung (Dewar, 2008). Research suggests that up to one-third of bullying behavior is carried out by bully-victims (Marini & Dane, 2010).

As noted earlier in this key, kids who bully often thrive on the ability to control others and may come to view volatile peers as puppets on a string. In this real-life relational bullying incident at a suburban elementary school, note how two young girls who crave popularity aim to elevate their social status by manipulating a volatile classmate.

What the Adults Witnessed

Third-graders Jada and Liza were swinging together on the playground during recess when their classmate, Riley, approached and asked if she could swing with them. They invited Riley to take the third swing, but just as Riley got going at full speed, the two girls brought their swings to abrupt stops and laughed together as they ran away from the swing set. Jada turned her head and shouted, "We're going over to the track, Riley. Have fun swinging."

Confused, Riley impulsively jumped from her swing, landing hard on the ground. She reached down, as if in pain, to rub her left ankle, which had buckled upon landing. Riley quickly got back up on her feet, however, and raced toward the track, to catch up with her classmates. When Jada and Liza noticed Riley approaching, they abruptly veered away from the track. Undeterred, Riley caught up to her classmates and said something to them, pointing to the track. Jada and Liza looked at each other and began to laugh again before continuing to walk away from Riley.

As soon as the girls turned their backs, Riley reached out and grabbed hold of the long scarf wrapped around Liza's neck. With a quick yank, she physically turned Liza around to face her, then grasped the second end of the scarf. Riley pulled both pieces of the scarf in opposite directions, effectively choking Liza. This lasted for under five seconds before Jada's screams for help caught a playground aide's attention and immediate intervention. Riley was quickly pulled away from Liza and marched to the office of the school's guidance counselor. Liza was shaken by Riley's actions, but unharmed.

What the Adults Did Not Witness

First, some background information on the girls:

Riley is a bright but socially awkward 8-year-old girl, diagnosed with Asperger's syndrome. She longs to be friends with her classmates but often finds herself excluded from games and activities due to behaviors that her classmates find quirky and sometimes even gross. Riley feels an intense degree of confusion, frustration, and humiliation over repeated incidents of peer exclusion and, on more than one occasion, has gotten into trouble at school for losing control of her emotions and lashing out verbally and/or physically at her peers.

Jada and Liza are best friends. They are in the same third grade class as Riley. Both girls cite "being popular" as one of their biggest wishes. To Jada and Liza, Riley's predictable emotional outbursts are a source of amusement. The socially savvy girls have intuited that they can elicit over-the-top responses from Riley—effectively controlling her like a puppet—through subtle actions that schoolteachers and aides easily overlook or fail to notice. Jada and Liza understand from experience that while Riley will get into trouble for her outbursts, they will actually experience a boost in their social status, as silent bystanders watch how they control Riley yet remain blameless in the eyes of unaware school personnel.

The Incident

Each day during the week prior to the scarf incident, Jada and Liza made arrangements with Riley to meet her at the swings during recess. To Riley, this plan made her feel important and desirable as a friend. She looked forward to the connection each day. Yet day after day, when Riley would arrive at the

swings, Jada and Liza would make a point of abruptly aban-
doning her, leaving her alone on the playground. For the first
three days of the week, Riley didn't fully catch on to the fact
that a cruel joke was being carried out at her expense. On the
fourth day, however—fueled by a painful landing on her ankle
and two back-to-back experiences of watching Jada and Liza
laugh whenever they looked at her—Riley suddenly understood with clarity that she was the object of intentional ridicule. In that moment of realization, she snapped.

Volatile children are particularly easy marks for socially astute kids
who take pleasure—and gain social status—from provoking intense emotional outbursts. When bullying is disguised as friend-

---

Exercise: Tapping the Strengths
of Vulnerable Kids

In looking at the question of who is bullied, we focus on various vulnerabilities of young people. In truth, however, all young
people possess personal strengths and unique abilities that enable
them to cope successfully with bullying. Building upon these
strengths is key to effective intervention.

Think about the young people that you know—students in
your classroom, clients you work with, children of your own. Consider each person's relative vulnerability to being bullied. For each
person you are concerned about, ask yourself these three important questions:

1. What personal strengths and unique abilities does this child
   possess?
2. What can I do to build this child's resilience in the face of
   potential bullying?
3. Who can be a part of this child's social support network—
   positive peers, supportive parents, attuned counselors, and
   so on?

ship, and friendship is used as a weapon (Whitson, 2011a), kids like Riley are left feeling confused, frustrated, humiliated, and unsure of how to cope, while frenemies like Jada and Liza remain free and clear to carry out their hidden aggression time and time again. In the next key, we revisit the incident between Riley, Jada, and Liza to study how adults can intervene to get to the root of the aggression and to thwart this type of bullying.

Signs a Child Is Being Bullied

As a child and adolescent therapist, a national educator on bullying, and, most importantly, as a mom, I would love to believe that any child—particularly my own—would feel comfortable enough to come to me if they were being bullied. The devastating reality, however, is that most kids do not readily reach out to adults for help during incidents of peer victimization. As we will see in Key 2, there are several real and powerful reasons that kids choose not to reach out to adults. A young person's reticence notwithstanding, it is critical that adults become astute in recognizing the warning signs that a young person is being bullied, so that they can intervene promptly—long before most kids are willing to come forward to talk about their experiences of pain and humiliation.

Signs that a young person may be the target of bullying include any of the following:

- Unexplained injuries
- Loss of property
- Destruction of clothing, electronics, and so on
- School avoidance
- Physical symptoms such as stomachaches, headaches, and so on
- Changes in eating, sleeping, grades, and such
- Avoidance of social interactions
- Drop in self-esteem and self-confidence
- Changes in mood: appearing sad, angry, or anxious after school
- Helplessness, hopelessness
- Self-destructive behaviors

Sadly, these signs very closely mirror lists of symptoms of suicidal behavior in young people. A young person who talks about suicide, self-harm, running away from home, feeling helpless, and/or blaming himself for being bullied should be evaluated by a professional.

When Does Bullying Take Place?

Speak the words "middle school" to any adults and listen for the groan to come out of their mouths. Watch their eyes roll. This developmental period elicits a visceral response from adults who recall with horror the awkwardness of their own adolescence and dread the thought of teaching, coaching, counseling, parenting, and observing their own kids through these years.

Part of the pain of the middle school years is that bullying appears to peak during this time. Filmmakers Lee Hirsch and Cynthia Lowen, creators of the acclaimed 2012 documentary *Bully*, attribute this intensity to the growing importance of popularity and peer acceptance, the increasing complexity of relationships, and the greater sophistication of kids in their wielding of social power (Hirsch & Lowen, 2012). Combined with surging hormones, bodily changes, and ever-expanding access to ever-evolving technology, these years are ripe for bullying of all kinds.

That's not to say that bullying begins and ends during the middle school years, however. Most professionals and parents can cite painful incidents of bona fide bullying from their kids' earliest school years, with searing memories of innocence lost and confidence shattered. A questionnaire developed by researchers at Lucile Packard Children's Hospital and the Stanford University School of Medicine revealed that 9 out of 10 elementary students experienced bullying at the hands of their peers and nearly 6 in 10 children surveyed reported participating in some type of bullying themselves (Stanford University Medical Center, 2007).

One note on the challenge of aggregating statistics on bullying across different age groups: As kids age, they become less and less likely to report incidents of bullying to adults. Fear of retribution and further social ostracism prevents older kids from talking to adults about incidents of peer cruelty. It is therefore even more important as young people progress through the later school years that adults remain vigilant for signs that bullying is taking place and maintain open lines of communication so that kids believe that it is okay to reach out for help in navigating troubling peer dynamics.

Whose Responsibility Is It to Stop Bullying?

Before I begin to answer this final question in Key 1, I want to state my unequivocal support for most educators, clinicians, counselors, youth workers, and parents working and living with young people. I am one of you. I have had the distinct honor of working with you in a professional capacity, and have exchanged stories with dozens of you through my own children's schooling. I recognize your role as monumental. It is my belief that most adults who dedicate their professional and personal lives to kids are heroes and I thank you endlessly for all that you do.

With that said, there are also adults who blatantly and callously fail children and I can't help but find it infuriating. While I understand that kids are often mean to each other—and sometimes unspeakably cruel—what I cannot wrap my mind around is when adults knowingly allow it to happen. Bullying is neither an inevitability nor a normal part of childhood, but rather an unnecessary form of aggression that attuned and caring adults have the power to put an end to.

In this final section, I acknowledge the obstacles faced by adults in stopping bullying while honoring the opportunities they have to make a positive difference in the lives of young people.

Never-Ending to-Do Lists

While I am of the conviction that adults are responsible for keeping kids safe, I am equally convinced that educators today have so much on their plates that safeguarding kids' emotional well-being is a real challenge. Differentiated instruction has classroom teachers bending over backward to meet students' unique learning needs while standardized testing mandates that common standards are achieved by all learners. Budgets are slashed and teachers are challenged to do more with less. Lesson planning, paper grading, test writing, parent conferences, student conferences, in-service training, answering e-mails, integrating technology, piloting new curricula: Have I even scratched the surface of all of the demands on a teacher's time? Oh, did I neglect to mention educating young people on that list? The to-do lists of teachers are never ending and anyone who dismisses the intensity of these demands is doing a disservice to educators and kids alike.

Nonetheless, be clear: School personnel have a responsibility to create a culture in which bullying is unacceptable and to protect kids from physical and psychological harm. This to-do item is as important as any of the others on the list and it is a shared responsibility among principals, counseling and guidance staff, classroom teachers, and parents to make creating a caring climate a central priority of a school. There can be no "it's not my responsibility" on this one; all hands must be on deck and efforts must be coordinated and consistent between professionals and parents to stop bullying.

When young people are bullied relentlessly and without adult intervention, they have difficulty succeeding academically. For this reason alone (notwithstanding their moral obligation), bullying is a problem adults are duty bound to address. On top of that, it is important to note that stopping bullying in schools is now part of a teacher's legal obligation. In 1999, Georgia was the only state to have an antibullying law on its books. Now, due to heightened awareness about the impact of bullying on kids, 49 states currently have antibullying laws on the books. (Now that's what I call progress.) By law, teachers must address bullying in schools when they are aware of it—even when they are really, really busy.

The "Rite of Passage" Mentality

Up to this point, I am always sympathetic to the obstacles professionals and parents face in managing bullying effectively. When it comes to the "kids will be kids" or "rite of passage" mentality, however, my empathy comes to a screeching halt. Minimizing a problem is not what caring adults do; it is what manipulative bullies do.

Yes, kids can be mean. No, adults should never dismiss bullying as a normative or tolerable fact of childhood. When they do, they violate a child's trust and abdicate their role as responsible adults. Period.

Feeling Overwhelmed and Underresourced

Bullying among school-aged children is regarded as a widespread problem in the United States. If there was an easy solution, it would have been suggested and implemented long ago. You wouldn't be thinking about it and I wouldn't be writing about it. Bringing an end to bullying is a complex challenge that leaves many of us feeling overwhelmed. More often than they would care to admit, the adult who downplays an incident of bullying simply has no idea how to approach the problem.

School personnel have little funding and less time for lengthy in-service training, long incident reports, and emotional confrontations with parents, bullies, bystanders, and victims. Clinicians already bogged down by privacy policies, paperwork demands, and packed client schedules struggle to implement complex, protracted interventions. Parents feel the urgent need to relieve their kids' burdens, but feel ill equipped or underqualified to intervene.

That's the bad news.

The good news is that "big" solutions to the problem of bullying are trumped each and every day by the small, powerful acts that trustworthy adults can use to signal to individual kids that their dignity is paramount and that their safety will be prioritized. The hopeful news about bringing an end to bullying is that while no magic wand cure-alls exist, there are all kinds of simple, focused, quick, and accessible strategies that professionals and parents alike can implement to stop bullying. Best news yet: Most of these efficient strategies simultaneously serve to build positive relationships between kids and adults, thus contributing to environments in which bullying just plain fails.

The remaining seven keys in this book are dedicated to exploring and outlining these strategies, in ways that are readily applicable and usable for readers.

10 Practical Strategies to Know Bullying When You See It

1. Understand the differences between rude, mean, and bullying behavior. Intervene accordingly.
2. Educate kids about bullying so that they know what to pay attention to, what to confront on their own, and what should be reported to a trustworthy adult.
3. Know the warning signs of a child who is being bullied and a young person who is at her wits' end.
4. Seek to uncover what motivates an individual young person to bully others.
5. Make a plan for how a child's vital interests (e.g., control, social status) can be constructively met and how aggressive behaviors will be confronted and changed.
6. Identify students who are particularly vulnerable to being bullied and those who are most likely to bully others.
7. Create cultures of kindness by rewarding good citizenship.
8. Reject the mentality that "kids will be kids." Bullying is never a rite of passage for young people.
9. Assign at least one adult in your school to be sure that student concerns about bullying are addressed promptly, thoroughly, and with dignity.
10. Create a support system among school staff by asking professionals to be accountable to one another in responding effectively to bullying.

ESTABLISH CONNECTIONS WITH KIDS

Most educators and youth-serving professionals I know came to this type of work because we share in common with parents and caregivers a personal drive to make a positive difference in the lives of young people. Collectively, we understand that the key to doing this is establishing meaningful connections with kids.

Unfortunately, too frequently along the way, we become absorbed by professional obligations or bogged down by the day-to-day demands of managing a household. In grading this paper, completing that report and running both kids to their eighteenth appointment, activity, sport, commitment of the week, we find ourselves transformed from human beings into human doings. Tasks take up most of our time and personal connections with kids become a luxury we believe we cannot afford.

Don't believe it.

Connections with kids are the essential prerequisite for any growth and change an adult will be able to facilitate. Meaningful connections with a young person are based on trust and nurtured through consistent positive interactions. When a child perceives that the adults in his life are truly invested in his well-being and interested in his experiences, he is more willing to talk about what is going on in his life and to be open to adult feedback. Even better, kids who believe that adults are sincere in their intentions to help are also more forgiving of the inevitable flubs we make in trying to understand and relate to them. Young people don't care if we have all of the words exactly right or even if we sometimes give "out-there" advice that "would never work." What they do care about is that we care about them. Their radar is usually pretty precise. Adults going through the motions of a job and asking rote questions in order to complete a checklist will be dismissed on the spot. On the other hand, adults who give of their time, listen well, take kids seriously, and generally avoid "freaking out" will be accepted—and appreciated—in the long term.

In this key we will explore what it means and what it takes to establish the meaningful connections with kids that allow us to help bring an end to bullying.

Give of Your Time

Time: It's the elephant in the living room, so I'll talk about it first. I am time conscious to a fault—motivated by deadlines and energized by the challenge of getting it all done. The ever-scrolling to-do list in my head clicks away and I'll admit that I enjoy the compliments I receive for being efficient. Most of my biggest professional blunders and all of my worst parenting regrets, however, have come from not giving enough time to kids because I was rushing to get stuff done.

Believe me, I don't minimize the importance of stuff. Stuff keeps employers happy and ultimately, the completion of stuff pays the bills. But to be honest, the stuff I do in a day isn't even important enough for me to give it a proper name. And by the end of a day, I can scarcely recall all of the stuff I got done.

I do, on the other hand, remember the name of every young person with whom I have had the honor of working over the past fifteen years and I can tell you honestly that my best moments with each of them have occurred when I put aside my agenda and just tuned in to their needs. Likewise, as a parent, all of my laugh-till-we-cry moments with my children have occurred off schedule. It hasn't come easy for me, as a hard-core task-doer, but the rewards have been overwhelming—and humbling.

To my fellow Type A task accomplishers who automatically put up a wall whenever someone mentions making time, I want to acknowledge that I know where your doubts come from. I live it. The good news is that you don't have to give up all of the task completion that makes you good at your job and accomplished in the eyes of your employers. You just have to be open to putting those tasks on a shelf every once in a while, when a child is asking for your attention. As you and I both know, the tasks will still be there waiting for you when you come back to them. Kids, on the other hand, don't always linger after an adult has ignored or dismissed them. We're stuck with our tasks until they are completed but our kids grow up—and grow away—very quickly. Carpe diem.

Now, with all of that said and an urgency established, here's some happy news: Connecting with kids is about giving time, but it is not necessarily a time-intensive commitment. Many of the most impactful ways that adults forge lasting connections with kids occur in minutes rather than in hours. That point was made clear to me by a 9-year-old student who told me, in a voice that I can only describe as gleeful, that her teacher really liked her. When I asked her how she could tell, she explained, "She smiles at me every day when I walk into her room. It's so different from my teacher last year. She was always doing work and never even looked up before the second bell, except to remind us of anything we were doing wrong. I think the teacher this year really likes me!" A series of twirls and joyful shrieks later, it was plain to see how something as simple and brief as a warm acknowledgment from a teacher meant the world to that student. Indeed, her teacher had her at hello.

Is Time Enough?

Am I suggesting that all adults need to do is smile at kids and the issue of bullying will be solved? No, not at all. For kids caught up in troubling peer dynamics, the support they need from adults goes far beyond a 5-second facial expression. What I am suggesting, however, is that something as momentary and uncomplicated as a warm daily greeting from an adult is a foundation for establishing a more meaningful connection and can go a surprisingly long way in indicating to a young person that the adult is consistent, warm, and perhaps even trustworthy enough to confide in.

A veteran teacher from a suburban elementary school recently shared with me this transformational story about the difference one minute a day made for a shy, young, formerly bullied student:

> Andrew did not speak a word to his peers for the first two weeks of class. Even to me, he only spoke in one-word phrases—brief answers to direct questions, spoken barely above a whisper. Andrew did not have any type of speech, language, learning, or social disability. Rather, in his own words, he was "really shy." His mother explained to me that Andrew had been bullied relentlessly during his first two years of school and was terrified of what this school year would bring in terms of his peer interactions.
>
> As you can imagine, there are days in a school classroom when it is pretty nice to have a quiet student, but it is also clear that kids need to be able to interact with their peers and with the adults in the school. I knew that I had two choices with Andrew: I could either blast the kid for his refusal to talk or I could support him. All of my experience in the classroom led me to know that supporting him—and rallying his young classmates to do the same—was the only option that would lead to positive outcomes for any of us.
>
> So, starting very early in the school year, I gave Andrew the job of doing our daily lunch count. To do this job, Andrew had to poll his 20 classmates every morning on who was packing lunch and who was buying it in the school cafeteria. For the classmates who were buying lunch, he had to ask a second question: Would they purchase the regular entrée or the alternate meal?
>
> For the first several weeks of the task, I had to give Andrew abundant coaching. I taught him exactly what he needed to

say and we practiced several times how to go through the one-minute routine. We even rehearsed the process as a class and I taught each of my students how to make eye contact with Andrew, assure him that he was doing a good job, and to use patience if he hesitated. I knew that making the time to teach my students how to support one another was as valuable as any reading or writing lesson we were going to accomplish in the school year. I also knew that I had to do it early in the school year or my window of opportunity would narrow.

I remember so clearly Andrew's face as he stood before the class, taking deep breath after deep breath before he could utter even a word. I admit, there were days that in my head I was thinking, "Andrew, if you don't hurry up and get the lunch count, the cafeteria workers are going to yell at me! Now, get a move on already." But I steeled myself and, taking inspiration from a large group of 7-year-olds who were practicing all of the skills of patience, compassion, and kindness that we had rehearsed, I waited. Some days it took Andrew minutes to begin, other days he plunged right in, but never did he fail to complete the lunch count. By mid-October, we had a one-minute routine down pat.

There were days when other students begged me to allow them the chance to be the lunch counter. I couldn't do it. I knew it was a job that Andrew needed and it was his to keep all year. The kids understood.

At the end of the school year, our tradition is to do a show for parents in which each student gets on stage alone and talks briefly about his or her school year. Before the show, Andrew's mother took me aside and confided her nervousness over Andrew taking the stage. She reminded me of how badly he had been bullied by his classmates the year before and worried that the kids would laugh at him on the stage. I reminded her of all of the opportunities Andrew had had to stand before his peers all year long and promised her that he would have a class full of friends cheering for him.

Sure enough, Andrew got up on stage with the same

confidence that every other student did and spoke for 30 full seconds about his year. He had a rip-roaring, hooting and hollering group of classmates cheer him off the stage. He beamed. I want to say that it was a transformational moment, but in truth, Andrew's confidence didn't occur in an instant. It occurred because of a school year full of instances—truly just a minute a day—that helped this debilitatingly shy, frequently targeted kid become a genuinely supported, cheered-on member of our little community. Time. Well. Spent.

Exercise: Commit to Connect

Little things become big things when it comes to connecting with young people. What are the little things that you do to make kids feel valued, heard, and understood?

Make a list of at least three new things you can do to connect with the young people with whom you work and/or live. Commit to implementing these strategies each and every time you interact with kids.

What Happens if I Don't Give Time?

When kids feel alienated from adults, we are all in a whole lot of trouble. This statement applies to acts of youth violence across the board, many of which are beyond the scope of this book. Pertaining to the dynamics of bullying, this much is clear.

Without strong adult connections:

- Kids who bully act without the hindrance of disapproval from a grown-up who matters to them.
- Kids who are victimized feel isolated from sources of support and intervention.
- Kids who witness bullying have no one to turn to to report what they have seen.

Meaningful connections with adults play an important role in both prevention and intervention in bullying. Kids who lack these connections benefit from neither.

For those who still worry that there is not enough time in the day to connect with each child, I submit that young people will get adult time one way or the other. It may be in positive ways, through our consistent, nurturing interactions, or it may be through their acting-out behaviors and crisis situations. The bottom-line question really is: How do you want to spend your time with a young person? A proactive investment of time in the development of a trusting relationship with a child is a whole lot easier (not to mention more time efficient) than a reactive response to a relationship gone awry.

Make It Easy for Kids to Talk About Bullying

One of the most insidious aspects of bullying is how it makes its victims feel isolated and alone. Many kids who are bullied are hesitant to talk about their experiences for these reasons:

- They feel burdened by self-doubt, wondering if some sort of personal defect is to blame for their victimization. To talk about their experiences would be to openly expose the part of themselves that feels inadequate.
- They feel humiliated and ashamed. The things that are said and done to them by their peers are bad enough, but to have to talk about it feels like a rewounding.
- They fear being branded tattletales by their peers and making an already bad situation even worse.

These fears are very real for a young person and make confiding in an adult about bullying quite scary. It is our responsibility to make it feel safe. In this section, we explore ways in which adults can make it easier for kids to talk about bullying.

Listen Well

When I began my career as an adolescent therapist, I was all of 23 years old. Though my clients weren't much younger than I was, there was a significant age difference between me and their parents. I felt inadequate about that gap—worried that my youth would be automatically interpreted as incompetence. To make up for this, I felt like I needed to have the answers for everything.

It was a valiant effort, if I do say so myself. (If nothing else, I did a lot of late-night re-reading of the *DSM* and my graduate school textbooks.) In feeling pressured to know everything there was to know about mental health and interventions, however, I neglected one very basic tenet of helping: honoring the fact that the client is the expert on his or her own life.

The need to overcompensate for my youth drove me to talk a lot during my early sessions with kids. The wisdom of experience taught me to be much quieter.

Listening, I learned, is a gift that adult helpers can give to young people. The experience of being heard and understood is profound for anyone, but particularly for kids who are accustomed to being on the receiving end of adult lectures. What does good listening "sound" like? In truth, listening should sound a whole lot like silence, only a bit more complicated. Listening well involves elements such as:

- *Complete attention and focus.* Real listening means that cell phones, computers, technology, personal agendas, and other distractions are temporarily put aside.
- *Good eye contact.* This is not to be mistaken with demanding that kids look adults in the eye when they are speaking, however. That social skill is for a different place and time. When kids are talking about painful material, it can be very difficult for them to make direct eye contact with adults. The responsibility for maintaining good eye contact lies with the listener. That said, one of the best places I listen to kids is in the car while I am driving, with my eyes glued to the road. There's just something about be-

ing trapped in a vehicle together without the intensity of eyeball-to-eyeball conversation that makes kids more apt to share.

- *Open-mindedness.* When adults believe that they know what a child is about to say, they listen differently than when they have an open mind about where the conversation will go. Effective listening means doing your best to clear your mind of already-drawn conclusions and keep pace with the child's perceptions, thoughts, and feelings about an event.

- *Open-ended questions.* Some kids can talk and talk and talk about bullying; others have more trouble getting started. Listening well may involve asking open-ended questions that prompt a reticent child to begin telling her story or help a confused one consider a new perspective.

- *Support and empathy.* It takes a lot of courage for young people to talk about their experiences with bullying. By the time a child has gotten beyond self-doubt, humiliation, shame, and the fear of being labeled a tattletale to tell an adult about bullying, chances are he is in a very painful place. Listening well involves affirming that child for having the strength to reach out and supporting him in what he has been through. Empathy is the gift of making that child feel understood and letting him know that from this point forward, he will not go through his experiences alone.

Listening and Solving Are Different

Often, a helping adult's first instinct when a young person confides about a bullying situation is to fix the problem. In her book *Queen Bees and Wannabees*, Rosalind Wiseman (2009) advises against this well-intentioned but misguided response, advising adults instead, "Don't just do something, stand there!" Listening well does not necessitate rushing in to solve all of a young person's troubles single-handedly, but rather implies a process in which an adult guides the youth to think through the steps needed to improve the situation. Some kids need more guidance than others about constructive solutions, depending on such factors as their age, intellect, and the particular dynamics of the situation, but all kids benefit from knowing that an adult has faith in their ability to think independently and manage problems competently.

How to Respond to a Child Who Talks About Bullying

Okay, the hard part is over; you have successfully established a meaningful connection with a child through which she has been able to overcome her fears and confide in you about a bullying situation. Congratulations! I mean this sincerely; this is no small feat. Now, what do you say in response?

For many adults, finding the right words can be a challenge. We may find ourselves in a bit of a panic, especially when the situation is particularly horrifying or has been going on for a long time. Our minds race with thoughts about the young person's safety, our own culpability, the school's legal responsibility, the sheer nerve of the child(ren) who perpetrated the bullying, frustration, confusion, exhaustion, and so on and on.

Maintain Calm

This brings me to my first point; when a young person takes the leap of faith to talk to you about a bullying situation, stay calm. Avoid freaking out. The dynamics she describes may be very run-of-the-mill or they may be entirely appalling but, either way, your role as a helpful adult is to listen well and respond as if the situation is completely manageable. The steadfastness of your response will go a long way in shaping the child's attitude as the two of you begin to move forward toward solutions.

Express Sympathy

Next, it is helpful to express sympathy to the child. Something as simple as "I am sorry this is happening to you" goes a long way in signaling to the young person that the dynamics just described are not a normal part of growing up and that you feel badly that the child has been on the receiving end of cruelty. Plain, simple, honest, and effective.

Thank the Child

Third, thank the child for finding the strength to tell you about the incidents. Acknowledging the courage it takes to overcome fear, embarrassment, and self-doubt is an important affirmation. What's more, only when a child talks about a situation does an adult get the opportunity to help do something about it. This is also something to express gratitude for. An effective message may sound as simple as, "It takes a lot of courage for a kid to talk to an adult about bullying. Thank you for trusting me enough to tell me."

Encourage Problem Solving

The final important element when a child has confided a bullying situation is to initiate the empowering process of problem solving. Because it is helpful to give kids a sense of ownership and control over both problems and solutions, adults should offer encouragement, such as, "You do not have to go through this on your own. Let's work together to come up with realistic strategies for handling this," but let the young person take the lead in coming up with specifics.

That said, it is certain that some young people, brimming with anger and frustration, may come up with ideas that sound neither reasonable nor, well, legal. Other youngsters, accustomed to adults solving their every problem, may express resentment at being challenged to come up with solutions. In either case, the adult's job is to continue to support the child, listen to her ongoing thoughts and feelings, and consistently assure her that you will work together to come up with constructive solutions. Much of a child's frustration in a bullying situation has to do with feelings of helplessness. The adult's role is to assist the child in reclaiming feelings of power and control through this process of listening, supporting, affirming, and thinking through solutions.

Follow-Up

Last, following up with a child after a conversation about bullying is critical. Just as bullying is not marked by a single act of cruelty, neither can one helpful conversation between an adult and child usually solve the entire problem. The adult should be sure to check in with the young person consistently after their initial conversation to confirm the child's physical and emotional well-being, convey ongoing support, talk about how identified strategies are working, recalibrate ideas that were not helpful, and generally affirm the connection that has been established.

Make It Safe

The final step in making it easy for kids to talk about bullying has to do with safety. As noted previously, one of the primary reasons that kids tend not to confide incidents of bullying to adults is their fear of being branded a tattletale or regarded as a weak person who cannot handle problems independently. Indeed, creating an environment in which victims feel unsafe to report bullying is part of an aggressor's overall strategy; kids who bully purposefully make their targets feel isolated and alone.

Safe Reporting

Establishing a culture in which kids believe they are safe to reach out for help is the responsibility of all adults and a key strategy for bringing an end to bullying. In any school or youth-serving organization, it is important to establish multiple ways to receive and collect information about bullying. These methods should allow for anonymity when practical and confidentiality always. Kids need to feel that they can report bullying to adults without fear of retaliation and free from the burden of believing, "Things will only get worse if I tell."

Technology can be especially useful when it comes to facilitating the safe reporting of bullying incidents among young people. Smartphones now have apps that allow kids, parents, and professionals to communicate safely about unwanted aggression in schools and communities. Hotlines can be established to allow for reporting. Many schools routinely conduct surveys throughout the school year to anonymously gather information about bullying behavior. Make no mistake: The fear that kids who bully create in their victims is powerful and even the best available technology can be made off-limits by their physical and psychological intimidation, but the more adults can create multiple, safe, confidential opportunities for reporting, the less isolated kids will feel.

Telling Versus Tattling

Like fingernails running down a chalkboard, tattling is painful to the ears of most adults. Likewise, for kids, the tattler is often the subject of scorn. And yet young people need a safe and acceptable way to reach out to adults to report unwanted aggression. It is helpful for adults to draw a clear distinction between tattling, a behavior designed specifically to get someone else in trouble, and telling, a behavior designed to keep someone safe. How do you teach kids key differences between tattling and telling? How can you be clear in teaching a young person that telling an adult about bullying is not a mark of cowardice, but rather a bold, powerful way to connect?

Exercise: How Will You Make It Safe for Kids to Talk About Bullying?

On a personal level, what can you do to make yourself a safe person for young people to confide in about bullying? With a colleague or friend, share strategies for signaling to kids that you are an approachable, trustworthy, and safe adult to whom they can turn.

On an organizational level, what systems can you establish to make it safe for kids to report bullying dynamics? What will you do with information gathered about kids who bully? How will you use this information to convey to all kids that their physical and emotional safety will be prioritized?

Take Reports of Bullying Seriously

According to bullying prevention expert, Dr. Michele Borba (2009), 49% of kids report having been bullied during the school year but only 32% of their parents believed them. When kids find the strength to reach out to adults to talk about bullying, it is of the utmost importance that we take their reports seriously. Do kids sometimes confuse rude or mean behavior with bullying? Yes. Should we dismiss reports that we believe to be exaggerated? Never.

When a young person takes the leap of faith to report bullying, the helpful adult's role is the following:

1. Listen to the child. Make him feel heard and understood. This experience all by itself builds relationships. You have nothing to lose and everything to gain by hearing him out.
2. Believe the child. Keep in mind that for young people, perceptions are reality. The experience of not being believed by an adult is soul crushing and will prevent this child from reaching out in the future. This plays very nicely into the hands of kids who bully.
3. If the incident is better classified as an example of rude or mean behavior, this is an opportunity for the adult to educate the young person on key distinctions between the behaviors. Being knowledgeable in this area will help the child down the road as he makes decisions about when to engage adults and how to respond to his peers. Also, since rude and mean behaviors can evolve into full-fledged bullying if left unchecked, the fact that you have been informed early on and can intervene while a situation is still manageable should be viewed as an opportunity.

When kids know that the adults in their lives will take their concerns seriously, they feel safe enough to reach out for help in a timely way. Research by Davis and Nixon (2010) cites these key steps that adults should take to signal to kids that their reports of bullying are being taken seriously:

1. Welcome the report an as opportunity to bring about change.
2. Do everything possible to keep the incident from happening again.

3. Know that the victim needs nurturing from an adult.
4. Check back with the victim to see if things are getting better.
5. Make sure that every child feels connected to her peers by encouraging caring, compassionate kids to spend time with the victimized young person.

Exercise: Receiving a Report

Consider how you will ensure that a young person's report about bullying is taken seriously:

- How will you communicate to the child that her report is received and believed? How will you safeguard the confidentiality of reports of bullying?
- How will you protect the child from retaliation by aggressors?
- How can you use a child's report of bullying as an opportunity to enhance your connection with her?
- If you are working with young people in a school or other professional setting and receive an anonymous report about an incident of bullying, what will you do to follow up?

Responding to Adults Who Dismiss Reports of Bullying

This past summer, I received an e-mail from a mother whose child attends a school at which I was scheduled to give a bullying prevention presentation. In no uncertain terms, she warned me that if I was going to come in and tell the kids that it was okay for them to "tattle like crybabies every time someone called them a name," then I should not bother coming at all. It was one of those e-mails that I couldn't even finish reading the first time through—and then I couldn't stop reading later on, because I had to make sure I was understanding her message correctly.

After several re-readings of the note and a whole lot of deep breaths, I wrote back to the parent:

Dear Theresa:

Thank you for your e-mail and for sharing your concerns with me. I thought it might be helpful for me to share with you a bit about how I approach the subject of bullying with kids. Any good bullying prevention program recognizes that peer conflict is inevitable and that sometimes kids abuse their social status and power. My role is to help children become competent in handling conflict so that they don't feel that they need to go to an adult until after they have tried to handle situations constructively on their own.

On the other hand, there is tremendous power behind name calling, social exclusion, peer isolation, verbal harassment, and other instances of aggression among kids. Even in the early elementary school years, kids are already much more likely to hide instances of bullying from adults than they are to "tattle" on their peers, due to their overpowering fear of being labeled as a "crybaby" and experiencing further ridicule. When kids do have the strength to reach out to adults, it is absolutely our obligation to honor their courage through the simple act of taking their reports seriously.

That same day, I heard back from the parent. She had a new sense of calm and satisfaction. And so did I. I guess sometimes we all just need to feel heard—and to be taken seriously.

Take Parents' Reports of Bullying Seriously

It is important to note that these guidelines on how to take a child's report of bullying seriously apply equally well to how professionals should respond when they receive reports from concerned parents. With most parents, this is a no-brainer; caregivers only reach out for help when the issue is real and they are ready to work side by side with professional staff to bring an end to the bullying. There are other parents, however, who reach out to professional staff overzealously. At any perceived slight of their child, they call the school office, demand immediate appointments with teachers, and/or fill up the voice mailboxes of counselors with threats of legal action.

While these relentless reports can become irritating distractions for professionals, it is important for any adult to understand that in most instances, a caregiver's zeal comes from a place of fear. Parents are protective by nature. They ache when their children ache. They wish to protect their kids from any sort of pain. Their internal alarms roar when they hear a news reporter link a young person's suicide with his/her history of being bullied because they instantly equate this kind of tragedy with the conflict their child is experiencing at school.

Sometimes parents overreact. Sometimes they perceive bullying when what really occurred is an incident of rudeness or rough play, like the "leaf incident" from Key 1. Other times, however, parents have their pulse on something very disturbing and dangerous that is going on under the radar of professionals. In any case, what is certain is that parents benefit from feeling heard and understood in the same way that children do. Parents, like kids, deserve to know that their concerns are being taken seriously. Adults, like children, can sometimes benefit from education on where meanness ends and bullying begins. In short, caregivers need to feel connected to professional staff just as much as kids do and when this connection is achieved, adults put themselves in an ideal position to work together toward bringing an end to difficult peer situations.

In Key 8, I outline specific strategies parents can use when their reports about bullying are downplayed by professional staff.

10 Practical Strategies to Establish Connections With Kids

1. Put aside your to-do list when kids enter your room. Greet them with a smile and speak to them by name.
2. In class, allow time to check in with kids on their emotional well-being. Kids need to feel safe in order to learn.
3. Make kids feel like you are crazy about them (in a good way).
4. Validate the experiences of bullied kids by listening to their stories.

5. Believe a child when he talks to you about bullying.
6. Connect each student with at least one adult in school whom she knows she can talk to about bullying.
7. Eat lunch with small groups of kids; demonstrate that you care about their everyday lives.
8. Use one-minute check-ins with your most vulnerable kids to find out how they are doing on any given day.
9. If you witness bullying, follow up with the child privately as soon as possible after the incident.
10. Establish multiple, confidential, safe ways for students to report bullying to trustworthy adults.

STOP BULLYING WHENEVER YOU SEE BULLYING

Strategies for Effective Intervention

Put aside for just a moment that I have been making the case that "big solutions" are not the way to bring an end to bullying. I promise to get back to that. First, though, it is important to begin this chapter by affirming that in order for adults to be effective in stopping bullying, we need to view the problem through a shared lens. If a teacher sees bullying everywhere, but his principal disagrees and can't identify it anywhere, we have a problem. Likewise, if a clinician is concerned that his young client is being victimized by her peers but the child's parents don't see the problem as worthy of intervention, we reach a standstill. In either scenario, the young person loses. Establishing a consistent, organization-wide understanding and approach to the issue of bullying is the very first step to intervening effectively.

Establish a Consistent Approach

Local communities, schools, and organizations are increasingly receiving a framework for how to approach bullying from their state governments. In 1999, just one U.S. state (Georgia) had an antibullying law on its books. Currently, 49 states do. Now that's what I call progress.

Antibullying legislation at the state level has laid the groundwork for local communities, schools, and organizations to develop specific policies that clearly define unacceptable behaviors, specify desirable ones, and outline discipline procedures. Perhaps even more importantly, legislative attention has shed light on the wide range of behaviors that fall under the bullying umbrella. Whereas the gold standard of this behavior was once limited to physical violence, adults now know for certain that cyberbullying and relational aggression can be just as painful and even more destructive.

It wasn't an easy task to establish a legal consensus on bullying from state to state, but now that it has been done almost everywhere in the United States, adults can move forward with a common understanding and shared objectives: identifying bullying

---

Exercise: How Do Your Antibullying Policies Fit With State Law?

If you have not had the opportunity to do so already, research your state's laws on bullying. How far does your state go in defining bullying, outlining antibullying procedures, recommending discipline, and funding prevention programs?

Look into how your school, organization, or community is governed by legislation at the state level. Does it have a set of written policies and procedures related to bullying? How are staff trained in this approach? Do you feel that this training is sufficient? Helpful? Realistic?

Well-conceived policies and procedures can be tremendously helpful in establishing a consistent framework for approaching an issue. Poorly planned ones can be cumbersome and may dismiss the reality that when working with human beings—and kids in particular—one size rarely fits all. What do you see as the strengths of your statewide and local antibullying laws? Where do you see room for improvement? What can you do in your role to adapt big, statewide approaches to your local, daily work with kids?

---

swiftly and responding to it promptly. (More on how to do these coming up in this key.)

Where do state and local governments still have a long way to go? Funding for antibullying initiatives. Antibullying advocates have made significant progress in getting legal definitions established and initiatives proposed, but the major frustration for educators, clinicians, youth workers, and parents is getting the dollars needed for training, implementation, and support of outstanding bullying prevention programs.

Now, as promised, we return from the big-picture look at state legislation regarding bullying to explore where bullying typically takes place in our own schools, organizations, and communities and what we can do to effectively stop it.

Where Does Bullying Take Place?

According to the National Center for Learning Disabilities (Horowitz, 2013), school personnel are reported to notice or intervene in only 1 out of every 25 incidents of bullying.

"How can this be?" you may wonder.

Easier than it seems, I am afraid. While most teachers are very focused on what goes on in their classrooms, up to 75% of bullying incidents in school occur in locations like the lunchroom, locker room, playground, bathroom, hallways, the bus and, perhaps most infamously, online. When professionals tell concerned parents that they are not aware of bullying incidents taking place in their classrooms, they are usually being honest.

That's not to say that bullying doesn't sometimes happen right under a teacher's nose. While physical bullying is usually fairly easy to observe and verbal bullying is easy enough to hear, one of the things that makes relational aggression so insidious is its hidden-in-plain-sight nature. This type of social bullying is characterized by things left unsaid and invitations not given. Its excruciating hallmark is silence. Relational aggression is a crime of omission that makes it very hard for even the most astute adults to catch it happening or be aware that it is taking place. Only through meaningful connections with individual students do professionals usually become aware of repeated, planned incidents of rumor spreading and exclusion. Only by really listening to kids' experiences can parents tune in to the pain that kids feel at being socially ridiculed and ostracized.

Increase the Presence of Connected Adults

Because the majority of bullying occurs outside of the classroom, one thing that makes a real difference in schools and treatment programs is to increase the presence of watchful adults in common areas. This is not to suggest an expensive big brother approach in which additional staff are hired or kids are watched like hawks at every moment of the day. Rather, schools and treatment programs can:

- Place observant teachers in the hallways between classes
- Station trained recess aides on the playground at recess
- Put knowledgeable monitors on the buses before and after school
- Assign astute food service workers to mingle with students in the cafeteria at lunch

At the end of Key 2, I included "Eat lunch with small groups of kids; demonstrate that you care about their everyday lives" as one of the 10 practical strategies. The same intervention that helps adults connect with kids also applies in this chapter. When adults are present in the cafeteria—not just as warm bodies picking up dropped napkins, but as integrated members of the student body—opportunities for bullying are diminished.

Any and all of the actions listed above, in fact, are effective both because they contribute to adult connections with kids and because they reduce a bully's opportunity to act. The increased physical presence of adults in common areas lets vulnerable kids know that adults are actively engaged in keeping them safe wherever they are. What's more—for the budget minded—these interventions use existing staff resources, rather than adding a line item for new funding.

Exercise: Where Should Adults Be?

It is true that adults cannot be everywhere or ever-present in the lives of young people. Where, specifically, should they be in your school, organization, or community to strategically lower the incidence of bullying behavior? Make a list of the top three to five locations. Share them with your team members as, together, you work to diminish the opportunities for bullying to take place.

If you are working in a school or educational setting, make a plan to change at least one thing about how adults are utilized in each of the following high-risk locations for bullying:

1. School hallways
2. Locker rooms
3. Bathrooms
4. Recess
5. Bus

For example, during transition times between classes, teachers will stand in the hallways or walk through them to check in with students, check on vulnerable kids, and establish an aware adult presence throughout school common areas.

Create a Positive School Climate

Because young people typically spend 7–10 hours per day, usually five days per week, either traveling back and forth to school or in their school environment, these next two sections focus on how school personnel and classroom teachers can effectively intervene to stop bullying. Please note, however, that the strategies described here are widely applicable to treatment facilities, small group settings, and even family life.

Stopping bullying in schools begins by creating school cultures in which bullying is not tolerated. (That's not to be confused with suggesting that schools institute rigid zero-tolerance policies. Rather, in Key 7 I talk about why zero-tolerance discipline actually tends to worsen bullying problems.) Positive school cultures are marked by concrete actions taken by adults to champion acceptance, honor diversity, foster cooperation, establish connections with kids, and facilitate open communication among staff and students.

Creating a positive school culture begins with the leadership of the principal and is maintained through the commitment of administrative and teaching staff. To be effective, bullying prevention must be a real priority for these adults, not just lip service given at a back-to-school night or a pledge handed out for students to sign. Likewise, fostering a positive school culture goes far beyond the hanging of "Bully-Free Zone" posters and its impact endures much longer than the once-and-done school assembly — no matter how dynamic or engaging the speaker (and I say that humbly, as one of those speakers). Effective interventions at the school level are integrated into the daily activities of staff and students and become a part of the way each person thinks, feels, and behaves toward others.

I know I risk sounding pie-in-the-sky when I say all of this, but the reality is that this kind of school climate can be created and is thriving at schools all over the country. At the school level, adults can create a school climate that is friendly to students and intolerant of bullying:

1. Establish bully prevention as a primary focus area. For schools using Positive Behavior Interventions and Supports, prioritize desired kid behaviors such as "Be respectful to others" as schoolwide goals and have connected adults consistently reinforce them.

2. Support specific interventions by school leadership to stop bul-

lying. For example, encourage the use of social and emotional learning (SEL) programs for all students, which have been shown to reduce bullying by up to 50%. (I talk more about SEL programs in Key 5.)

3. Empower kids to stand up for each other and teach and encourage good bystander behavior. (Specific strategies for empowering bystanders are covered in depth in Key 6.)

4. Popularity among the student body should be defined more by being well liked than by being socially feared.

5. Establish buddy systems. Students from upper grades watch out for younger students and kids high on the social status ladder are paired with more vulnerable kids.

6. Keep open lines of communication between staff and students. Reporting bullying should not be a scary, intimidating process for a young person, but rather a comfortable extension of regular conversations he has with familiar teachers, counselors, and administrative staff.

7. Adults should encourage diverse and dynamic friendship groupings by intentionally separating and mixing up cliques and exclusive groupings of kids.

8. Celebrate differences and honor diversity.

9. Responding to bullying takes precedence; adults take reports seriously and address issues before they escalate and become more difficult to manage.

10. The school goes beyond teaching tolerance and instead champions acceptance. What schools don't tolerate, on the other hand, is bullying of any kind.

Create a Positive Classroom Culture

Teachers play the pivotal role in a school's efforts to bring an end to bullying. Duly credited as the shapers of young people's minds, classroom teachers are also the sculptors of peer ecologies. Rodkin and Hodges (2003) cite evidence that when teachers are warm and caring to their students, the students, in turn, become less rejecting of their peers. This is a real "do as I do" opportunity for classroom teachers.

Make Kindness a Classroom Norm

Teachers who are most effective in stopping bullying are the ones who work to create classroom cultures in which kindness is valued over coolness and popularity is based not on the power to dominate social interactions but rather on the willingness to reach out to others compassionately.

Recall the example of the painfully shy and relentlessly bullied young student, Andrew, in Key 2. His teacher noted that she had a choice to make: "blast" Andrew for his refusal to speak in class or support him in overcoming his reticence. She opted to dedicate one minute each morning to a routine school activity that became a foundation for a caring classroom community. For Andrew, it meant the difference between a school year of repeated peer rejection and one of genuine friendship and support. Ultimately, it was the difference between silence and finding his voice. For his 20 young classmates, it meant learning that compassionate kindness and patience are as much a part of their daily routines as eating lunch and learning to read.

How else can teachers foster a kind and supportive school environment in which bullying behaviors cannot find roots?

- Classroom meetings, activities, and discussions can shape a student's beliefs about what it means to be cool.
- Group rules and classroom norms dictate that cruel behaviors have a social cost.
- SEL is incorporated into everyday lessons so that students have regular opportunities to practice bully-banning behaviors such as compassion and empathy.
- Cooperative group work trumps competitive interactions.

The list goes on, but the key is that effective teachers are incorporating bullying-prevention strategies seamlessly into the culture of their classroom. There is no special assembly or crisis-inspired group talk to focus on antibullying efforts; rather, every action, every day is shaped by norms of kindness.

Reach Out to Vulnerable Kids

Teachers who create positive classroom cultures make it a habit to reach out to students who are vulnerable to peer rejection and exclusion. Case in point: last year, the mother of a socially awkward but eager-to-please middle school student came to me concerned that her daughter's teacher was actually contributing to the exclusion her daughter was experiencing at school. She described an incident in which the students were permitted to divide themselves into small groups to work on a project. Her daughter, Katie, was not invited to join any of the groups. When Katie asked to be included, her classmates unanimously informed her that their groups were already full. When Katie asked her teacher to help her find a group, the teacher walked Katie over to a group of popular girls and announced apologetically, "I'm sorry, girls. Katie will have to be in your group." When one of the group members rolled her eyes, the teacher put her hand reassuringly on the angry girl's shoulder and said, "You'll be okay. It's only for this week."

The mother was outraged. Her daughter was humiliated. I could have cried. And yet it's nowhere near the first time I have heard this kind of story of an adult overidentifying with kids who bully and allowing acts of exclusion to go on unchecked.

Effective teachers do not cater to the social hierarchies established by popular students, nor do they sympathize with the inconvenience students feel at having to work with an awkward peer. Rather, teachers who are successful in stopping bullying are those who encourage classmates to rally around the vulnerable peer in distinctive, meaningful ways. Organizing a group cheer so that the classmate with autism smiles for his school photo, establishing a buddy system that pairs a socially successful student with a socially vulnerable one, and staying involved in the seating arrangements at lunch so that each child has at least one, guaranteed friendly peer with whom to sit are among the least time consuming, yet most impactful things effective teachers do to reach out and meet the needs of at-risk students.

Use Brief Messages

Think back to your childhood for a moment. Recall something that an adult said to you—either good or bad—that has always stuck in your mind. Before moving on, reflect on the impact that that message has had on your life, your way of thinking, and your actions.

The messages that adults give to kids have a way of becoming internalized as part of a child's own inner voice. Ideally, young people are receiving positive messages from adults that shape their thinking in constructive, esteem-building ways. One particularly effective teacher I know describes her commitment to using specific, memorable, meaningful brief messages with all of her students as a strategy for creating a positive mind-set and optimistic classroom climate. Literally each and every day, she uses specific messages such as these:

- Life is great.
- Crayons will break. (*The elementary school version of "accidents happen."*)
- I can do it.
- Be known for being kind.
- Keep everyone in the heart.

Her students often string together the long sequence of letters "LIGCWBICDI" on their homework and test papers. To uninformed onlookers, the letters look nonsensical, but to young minds in the know, they are an important affirmation of the messages they are internalizing—that life is great, crayons will break, and they can do anything they set their minds to.

Specific to bullying prevention messages, the teacher explained the last phrase on the list above, saying that she once was telling her students that their classroom was like a great big heart, when one of the kids shouted out, "Yeah! And we're all in it!" Starting at that moment, as a group, they spontaneously adopted the new phrase, "Keep everyone in the heart." From that point forward, that brief message was added to the list and became a gentle, student-initiated reminder anytime a classmate began to do or say something hurtful.

More efficient than an after-the-fact lecture and more impactful than reactive warnings spoken with anger, positive brief messages play a proactive role in preventing cruel behavior among young people. Consistently used helpful phrases become part of a young person's inner dialogue and impact the way kids think about themselves in relation to the world. They can be a powerful part of any adult's daily bullying prevention routine. Consider for a moment: What enduring messages would you like to impart to a child?

Intervene on the Spot

Not long ago, a teacher confided in me that he felt very confident about the bullying prevention training provided by his school district as far as protocols for identifying bullying behavior, but he always found himself at a loss for words when he was face-to-face with a bullying situation between kids. "I don't know what to say to make it stop," he confessed.

This teacher is not alone. Many adults struggle with crafting just the right message to deliver to kids when they witness an incident of bullying. The good news is that just like the brief messages noted above, often the most effective approach to stop bullying on the spot is the least wordy one. In fact, in most cases, I say, the briefer the better. Each of these statements below would take less than 15 seconds to deliver:

- "It's not okay to say that to someone in my classroom. Are we clear?"

- "Sending that kind of text about a classmate is unacceptable. That cannot happen again."
- "Leaving one kid out of the group is not going to work. Let's fix this and move on."

The benefits of these brief statements?

- They don't humiliate or alienate anyone.
- They do let everyone know that the teacher is astute, aware of classroom dynamics, and not afraid to step in.
- They send a strong signal to all students that bullying behavior will not be tolerated.
- They assure the kid who is bullied that she has a safe place and a trustworthy adult in the school.

These uncomplicated statements also have the distinct advantage of allowing a teacher to get right back to the lesson while simultaneously heading off all kinds of future issues from occurring on his watch.

Exercise: How Would You Respond?

Each of the following examples is a real-life incident reported by teachers. Read each example and craft a brief response to the students involved. (While there is no single correct response to any of the scenarios, a suggested response is provided for each one at the end of the exercise, for your reference.)

Scenarios

1. You overhear a group of kids teasing one student about a drawing on his notebook. They are laughing together and repeating phrases such as, "That's so gay" and "What a gay cartoon."
2. You find out that a small group of kids in your class are looking at—and laughing about—a photo being passed around via cell phone of a female student's midsection. The caption on

the photo reads: "How many rolls can you count on Lindsey's stomach?"

3. You discover that a group of students are passing a survey around school to poll classmates: "Who is most likely to be a 40-year-old virgin?" When asked about it, the students say, "We were just joking. It's no big deal."

4. You overhear a small group of kids tell one student at lunch, "You can't sit with us."

5. You are told that a fake Facebook page has been set up about one of your students. The page was set up by a group of three students in your class and features lewd language and photos designed to humiliate and shame the targeted student.

Possible Responses

1. "It is not acceptable to use those words to put someone down. Are we clear?"

2. "Sharing that kind of photo about a classmate is unacceptable. Delete it right now while I watch. Are we good?"

3. "I can take a joke but what you have here is not funny. It's not okay to ask questions that are designed to embarrass or humiliate others. This goes in the trash right away and there will be no more surveys like this."

4. "Leaving one kid out of the group is not going to work. Let's fix this and move on."

5. "I understand that a fake Facebook page has been set up. I assume you know that this is illegal and punishable by law. I expect that the page will be taken down right away."

The knowledge that brief, on-the-spot interventions are more effective than long, schedule-disrupting, lecture-like encounters is a relief to many educators. Still, some worry that kids will just find a way to bully their peers at a later date and time. They are right to worry; chances are excellent that bullying will happen again.

It would be naive, in fact, for any adult to think that a single intervention would be enough to radically and permanently change the behaviors of a young person. As a normative part of their development, kids are exploring their social worlds and testing out new behaviors. They are actively seeking to find the limits of adults, the approval of their peers, and the length to which they can stretch their own values. One brief bully-interrupting intervention will not forever halt aggressive behavior by a child, but repeated, nonhostile, consistent intolerance for bullying can. Throw in steady reinforcement of kindness and you're well on your way to creating a positive classroom climate.

A Spot-on, On-the-Spot Intervention in a Sixth Grade Classroom

Here's a real-life example of how two sixth grade girls seized an opportunity to behave badly when their regular classroom teacher was away, and how the teacher addressed their meanness upon her return:

> Talia age 12, was upset on a Friday afternoon when she got home from school. She confided in her mother that two girls from her class were working on a list in school. The list included three distinct categories: Girls They Liked, Girls They So-So Liked, and Girls They Hated. While Talia did not specify where her name had been on the list, she knew the list making had hurt others and was feeling distraught over it.
>
> Talia's mother was unsure how to handle the situation. Since she couldn't determine if her own daughter had been cruelly victimized by the list and she wasn't sure if list making rose to the level of bullying, she wasn't sure if she should do anything about it. She asked me for my advice.
>
> Borrowing from the Olweus Bullying Prevention Program, my first bit of counsel was this: "If it is mean, intervene." Without knowing more about the list, its usage, how many

kids had seen it, and so on, it was impossible to determine if it was an example of mean behavior or full-fledged bullying but, in either case, it was clearly not contributing to positive classroom relationships and needed to be brought to a halt before it caused widespread or lasting damage.

Because the regular classroom teacher was not in school that day, the only way she would be able to do something about the creation of the list was if she knew about it. My second piece of advice to Talia's mother, therefore, was to be sure to inform the teacher as soon as possible, in order to give her the opportunity to intervene. Talia's mom sent an e-mail to the teacher that Friday afternoon. On Monday morning, she received a note back from the teacher, with thanks for bringing the situation to her attention and a promise to follow up with the students.

Just after gym that morning, the teacher asked all of the students in her class to settle in for a class meeting. She told them that she came up with a game that she thought would be fun.

"I am going to sort you into categories," she explained. "The categories will be Students I Like, Students I So-So Like, and Students I Really Don't Like."

Then she paused and looked around the circle. Most of the students looked shocked. Some of them turned red (the two girls involved mostly). The teacher asked the students, "Why wouldn't this game be a good idea?" For a solid 10 minutes, she entertained kids' endless stream of adamant responses about why the game was a bad idea for anyone to play.

The teacher also took time to talk about the typical things kids think about when they think of bullying (e.g., hitting, name calling, cyberbullying), then explained that there were other actions that could escalate into bullying such as gossip, whispering, exclusion, and, yes, list making. She acknowledged that sometimes spontaneous social situations arise and kids who get involved may not initially recognize them as bullying, but rather think of them as innocent fun. She cautioned them clearly, "The minute any kind of cruelty starts, the situation is no longer okay and must stop."

In the end, she told them that she did not think this game was necessarily a form of bullying but that it could have become a much larger and more hurtful issue. She instructed the students to destroy anything they had written that could be hurtful and told them that if she saw anything similar from that point forward, it would become an issue to share with their parents and the school principal.

The last thing the teacher did was key; she told the kids that although it isn't always easy to speak up when you know something is wrong, it is always the right thing to do. This closing message signaled to Talia that confiding in her mother was both brave and just and affirmed her trust that the adults in her world—both her mom and her teacher—would see to it that hurtful behavior was halted on the spot.

Adults who are making a difference in the movement to stop bullying are astute shapers of peer culture and engaged role models of kindness. They are champions of the underdog who are not afraid to directly confront bullying behavior whenever they see it. Educators, clinicians, and parents actively improve the lives of young people each and every day when they demonstrate that time spent on bullying prevention is time saved on conflict, alienation, academic struggles, and victimization.

10 Practical Strategies to Stop Bullying Wherever You See It

1. Draft a formal school policy on bullying that creates a clear and common understanding about what bullying is and how it will be handled.
2. Include staff and students on the committee to develop school policy on bullying. Share this policy with students via small group discussions.

3. Establish a hierarchy of logical consequences for bullying. Avoid zero-tolerance policies.
4. Establish a partnership with parents about school policies and protocols related to bullying.
5. Increase adult presence in common areas, including the cafeteria, hallways, locker rooms, recess, and bus.
6. Eat lunch with students. Station staff at particular tables in the cafeteria.
7. Be known for being kind in all of your interactions with young people.
8. Integrate bullying prevention activities into daily routines, such as class meetings, buddy systems, lunchtime seating arrangements, and so on.
9. Encourage classmates to rally around vulnerable peers in distinctive, meaningful ways.
10. Use brief, direct statements to stop bullying in its tracks and establish your classroom as a safe place for kids (and an unsafe place for bullying).

KEY 4

DEAL DIRECTLY
WITH CYBERBULLYING

It's a fact of life in the 21st century that kids are connected to each other 24-7. A generation ago, young people who were bullied in school could count on hours spent at home as a respite from ridicule. Today, kids are constantly connected through texting, instant messaging, and social media sites; sadly, there is little rest for the bully-weary.

Adults have made a giant misstep in recent years by choosing not to take responsibility for responding to aggression that occurs via technology. Why the widespread hesitation? School personnel back away, saying, "It didn't happen during school hours. . . . This isn't our problem. . . . There is nothing we can do." Local law enforcement maintains a distance until and unless a clear crime or serious threat to safety is evident. Parents—often digital immigrants in their kids' native cyberlands—throw their hands up, believing they lack the technological skills to keep up with what their kids are doing online. This across-the-board abdication of responsibility by adults has given kids who bully incontrovertible evidence that they are in charge and that their use of technology can control the culture of the peer group, free and unfettered by adult intervention.

One of the most important things that educators, clinicians, youth care professionals, and parents can do is to join together to deal with cyberbullying head-on, acknowledging its deep impact on a child's world and setting standards that hold kids accountable for their online behavior. In this key, we begin by examining the prevalence of cyberbullying among young people, then outline clear technology safety strategies for adults and kids alike.

What Makes Cyberbullying So Bad?

Hinduja and Patchin (2010) define cyberbullying as "when someone repeatedly makes fun of another person online or repeatedly picks on another person through e-mail or text message or when someone posts something online about another person they don't like." Based on this definition, their studies of kids ages 11–18 show that around 20% of kids say they have been victims of cyberbullying attacks and about 10% report being both a victim and an offender.

In the world of statistics, these numbers don't seem too terrible, do they? In truth, it would be easy for me (or you) to type "statistics on cyberbullying" into an online search engine and come up with far more alarming numbers—perhaps generated by much less rigorous researchers—but in fairness, the danger of cyberbullying is not in the breadth of perpetrators and victims, but rather in the depth of damage that a single incident can cause.

The Viral Nature of Cyberbullying

Cyberbullying often occurs alongside other "traditional" bullying methods but is distinct from physical, verbal, and relational aggression in these important ways:

1. Cyberbullying can occur anonymously, as perpetrators operate from behind computers and smartphones, rather than face-to-face. Kids believe they can get away with aggression without having to own up to it.
2. For many youngsters, anonymity is also a Get-Out-of-Guilt-Free card. Kids find it far easier to be cruel when they don't have to lock eyes with the object of their viciousness.

3. Pain becomes viral. Traditional bullying is usually a one-to-one encounter between a bully and a victim. While witnesses may be present, the size of a regular bullying audience is limited to who can fit in the hallway or listen in on a phone line. In cyberbullying, however, the potential audience is huge. Technology allows for almost endless forwards, shares, and "likes." No longer is a child the object of scorn for a few classmates; with technology, he can become humiliated throughout his school, community, and even worldwide. Mere keystrokes can create instant and almost unimaginable damage.

4. "What happens on the Internet stays on the Internet." Traditional bullying occurs as an event. It happens; then it is over. The pain lingers, no doubt, but the incident itself has a distinct conclusion. When a child is the victim of cyberbullying, on the other hand, his victimization can be repeated endlessly, as photos, videos, and messages are sent and resent. What's more, these posts remain on the Internet indefinitely. Even when a perpetrator apologizes for a cyber attack and takes down a cruel posting from its starting point, the item still exists—and can be forwarded—from any other site to which it has already been shared.

5. There are no time or space boundaries with cyberbullying. Whereas physical bullying requires two people to be in the same place at the same time, cyberbullying thrives on after hours and distance. A young person may be safely nestled at home with her family, while simultaneously under attack online by her peers.

Does Technology Cause Cruelty?

It goes without saying that bullying has been around for a lot longer than the Internet and cruelty among young people dates back much farther than smartphones. Bazelon (2013) points out that the way kids treat each other via technology is merely an extension of the way they treat each other when they are face-to-face—not a brand new or wholly different type of behavior. For all of the reasons noted above, technology does seem to exacerbate cruelty, but we can rest assured that it does not cause it.

Rest assured? Yes. This fact is truly good news for professionals and parents, because it reminds us that cyberbullying is not an untouchable behavior that only the current generation understands and can deal with. Rather, online aggression is something that any adult can help bring an end to. Today's kids need the focused, united, and comprehensive efforts of adults who are willing to address this danger directly.

Exercise: What's New in Bullying?

It is certain that abundant access to technology and constant connectedness online has added a new dimension to the culture of bullying. Consider:

- What are the specific challenges, brought on by technology, that today's young people face?
- How are they similar to the challenges you faced growing up?
- In what ways are they entirely distinct?
- How can you help kids overcome the challenges of living in an ever-connected world?
- What are the latest social media sites, apps, and venues that kids are using?
- How can you become well versed in these latest media, so that you can speak knowledgeably about them with kids and intervene effectively when needed?

At What Age Should Kids Start Learning About Online Safety?

Do you work in an elementary school and think you have a few years before you have to start worrying about cyberbullying? Are you the parent of a little one who can't possibly experience the dangers of texting and sexting since she doesn't own a cell phone yet? If you are the kind of adult who cares enough about kids and their safety to be reading this book, you instantly know that both questions are rhetorical. In today's world, with apps designed for infants and laptops marketed to preschoolers, we know that we need to prepare even our youngest kids to live safely online. What follows is an example of a sleepover among newly minted 10-year-olds that seemed so youthful and innocent at the time:

Eight fourth-grade classmates were together at Gigi's house for her tenth birthday sleepover party. They began their night as many partygoers do—eating pizza, watching movies, opening presents, and loading up on sweets. Gigi's parents were both involved in all of the activities—helping the girls make dinner, painting nails, chit-chatting, and rearranging furniture in the basement to make room for six sleeping bags, six pillows, and about three dozen stuffed animals. When the lights went out at 11 p.m., the scene looked like childhood personified.

When Gigi's parents went to bed, however, adolescence washed over the girls like a storm. Spearheaded by Hailey, a girl whose older siblings helped her become more "advanced" than the rest, conversations quickly moved into boys, then liking boys, then kissing boys, then taking photos at the sleepover to show to boys. The photos began when the girls were talking about bras and continued as they were trying on each other's bras. (No, not all of the 10-year-olds were wearing bras, but yes, those who were had on some very lacy—even racy—ones. That's a whole other book.)

The photos got worse as the girls got swept up in their own momentum. From bras to underwear, Hailey had the idea of trying on a pair of extremely short shorts. Another girl suggested she try them on without underwear. Then, a third girl took a photo on her cell phone of Hailey modeling the shorts.

Exhausted by their own silliness, the girls eventually fell asleep. In the morning, they ate pancakes and bacon, hugged their stuffed animals, and acted like 10-year-olds again. They went back to school as best friends and talked about that sleepover fondly for the rest of the year.

Four years later, as eighth graders, their friendships had changed. The eight girls were no longer a tight-knit group. Hailey, whose mature ways were admired when the girls were 10, was now the subject of one of middle school's worst forms of verbal bullying: slut-shaming. Friends and frenemies alike joined forces to call her names and humiliate her publicly. This went on for months and school had become almost unbearable for her. Hailey thought things had gotten as bad as they could get—until they got worse.

One day, a photo was posted on Hailey's Facebook page, with the caption, "Whoring around since the fourth grade." Hailey didn't recognize the photo at first. She was hurt and confused as kids from all across her middle school seemed to know about it. She was in full-fledged denial that the photo was even real, until one of her fellow sleepover fellow party-goers laughed and asked, "Remember that night at Gigi's? We all had so much fun!"

Indeed, that night in fourth grade did start off with childlike fun. Even when the topics started to veer off-color into boys and bras, there was still an innocence to it. The addition of technology to the mix, however, instantly changed that sleepover from a night young girls could remember fondly to an evening that Hailey would forever regret. Did the cell phone camera cause the cruelty? No. The picture taker's intentions at the time were pure. Did the use of technology create an unanticipated, long-term risk for the girls? Absolutely.

Be assured: It was not just Hailey who was put at risk. Although it was she who bore the brunt of intense ridicule when the photo was shared online, the girl who posted it also put herself in legal jeopardy. Having and posting photos of underage girls' private parts is a crime. In one impulsively cruel click of a mouse, a 14-year-old girl who thought she was just kidding around found herself in serious trouble with the law. The situation ended badly for all.

Could those girls have anticipated all of the trouble that was to come?

At 9 and 10 years of age, most kids are very aware of technology but still quite naive about all of the hurtful ways in which it can be used. Well into their adolescence even, many kids remain oblivious to the legal consequences of their online actions. One of the most important things that adults can do to bring an end to cyberbullying is to teach kids about the risks of their online behavior and to give them skills to protect themselves from lasting harm. This kind of education should begin as soon as kids start using technology or spending time with others who do. Bear in mind that Hailey did not own a cell phone—she merely attended a party with a friend who did. In this world, it is almost certain that waiting until kids have their own e-mail addresses, smartphones, social media profiles, and Facebook accounts is waiting way too long.

Technology Safety Strategies: What Professionals and Parents Can Do

While many professionals and parents feel like digital immigrants in a world ruled by young cybernatives, any lack of technological expertise on their part can usually be compensated for by their greater social and moral savvy. The technology safety strategies that follow provide practical, everyday steps that any adult—from tech wizard to cybernovice—can use to guide and protect kids when it comes to their behavior online.

Keep Person-to-Person Connections Strong

Peer-to-Peer Interactions

In our digital world where device-to-device communication dominates social exchanges, the best single predictor of healthy emotional interactions by young people is having lots of face-to-face communication (Bazelon, 2013). Parents are helpful in this area when they encourage kids to put away devices during social situations and engage with their peers in good, old-fashioned play. For younger kids, it is usually fairly easy to encourage imaginative, tech-free play. By as early as the upper elementary school grades, however, many kids are already wanting to integrate technology into their peer interactions. Playing video games, watching You-Tube videos, commenting on Facebook, sharing on Tumblr, and downloading the latest apps may seem like harmless ways for kids to spend time together, but caregivers do their kids a greater service by removing technology from the social mix and structuring situations in which kids interact face-to-face.

Adult-to-Child Interactions

Young people need to feel connected enough with adults offline to be willing to tell them about bullying incidents that occur online. Below, I talk about specific strategies adults can use to monitor kids' use of technology, but be clear: Even the most astute observers will miss some troubling online activity and no adult can keep tabs on all of the members of a child's social network. Cyberbullying expert Parry Aftab agrees that it is impractical for parents to be able to join and track all of a child's social networking and online activity, pointing out that the typical youngster has three to five Facebook pages, while their parents only know about one of them (Willick, 2013). The only viable option for adults who want to know what is happening online is to create a supportive daily environment in which young people feel safe enough to share.

Professionals and parents should broach the subject of cyberbullying directly with kids, teaching them first and foremost about healthy social relationships and treating others respectfully during online encounters and also to always let someone know about incidents of online aggression. For parents, it can be incredibly humbling to learn that your child's "someone" is not you. Try not to take it personally; your opinion means everything to your child and he or she may be too fearful of disappointing you to confide news about being bullied (or acting like a bully) online. As long as you have connected your child with at least one trustworthy adult that he or she can talk to, you have met a very important need.

Second, adults have a vital role in teaching kids about the legal ramifications of online cruelty. Grace's Law in the state of Maryland is a landmark cyberbullying bill, named for 15-year-old Grace McComas, who committed suicide after vicious harassment via social media. Whereas previous legislation in Maryland applied only to harassment through e-mail, Grace's Law expanded it to apply to bullying on social media sites as well. As more states follow suit, no longer will online cruelty be tolerated as a "thing kids do in their free time" and no more can young people—or the adults responsible for them—claim ignorance as a defense for their wrongdoing. Professionals and parents must take the responsibility for educating kids about the long-term legal and moral consequences of cyberbullying.

Adult-to-Adult Interactions

One of the most reliable ways that adults can become knowledgeable about incidents of cyberbullying is to stay connected with other adults. In order to come together to bring an end to online aggression, however, professionals and parents both must feel safe enough to give and to receive honest, sometimes hard-to-hear information about kids. This kind of safety is achieved when adult-to-adult interactions are grounded in a mind-set that "We're all in this together" rather than fueled by accusations of "Look what your terrible child did."

While most parents, myself included, crave the belief that "my child would never do that," the truth is that almost any child can get caught up in a moment of wanting to belong, an instance of poor judgment, or an episode of cruelty. Remaining open to this reality is critical. Sticking our heads in the sands of denial, on the other hand, precludes any adult's ability to guide, protect, and teach kids skills for stopping cyberbullying. The bottom line is: Kids make mistakes online. Our role as adults is to keep them from making the same bad mistakes over and over again and the way we do this starts with acknowledging when poor decisions are made, then giving kids guidance on how to make amends and stop the behaviors from reoccurring.

As hard as it can be for some parents to hear about their own child's cruel behaviors, it is even more difficult for other adults to be the bearers of bad news about an incident of cyberbullying. These adults worry about how they will be judged. They fear being accused of blowing a situation out of proportion. They don't want to be labeled a tattletale. Sound familiar? These worries are real, but as adults we must be strong enough to live with them. When adults are aware of cyberbullying but don't intervene, they are incompetent at best and complicit at worst. The only way that anyone can do something about cyberbullying is if they know about it. When adults fail to keep each other informed, we fail each other. We fail victimized kids. But we empower kids who bully. How backward is that?

In the following scenario, one parent approaches two other parents about a cyberbullying situation that impacts all of their daughters.

Kelli's mother is flipping through images on her daughter's Instagram account when she comes upon a photo featuring a zoomed-in shot of the rear end of one of Kelli's 14-year-old classmates. Kelli is among several people who have posted cruel comments about the photo, including comments like "Biggest ass in the class," "Eeew, gross. Fat bitch," and "How do you spell L-O-S-E-R??"

Kelli's mother is shocked by what she sees. She immediately confronts her daughter about the photo and supervises as the photo is taken down from the social media site and deleted from Kelli's cell phone. Kelli is also held responsible for closing down her Instagram account on the spot. The mother and daughter discuss all of the reasons why the photo was inappropriate to have taken in the first place, inexcusable to have posted online, and indefensible to have commented on so maliciously. For Kelli's mom, that was the easy part. Beyond that, she knew she had two difficult conversations yet to come: one with the unfamiliar parent of the classmate whose backside was featured online and one with a close personal friend whose daughter had also participated in the vicious online commentary. What follows are the dialogues she initiated with each family.

Conversation With the Unfamiliar Parent of the Targeted Teenage Girl

KELLI'S MOTHER: Hello, my name is Kate. I am Kelli's mother. Kelli is in class with your daughter.

CLASSMATE'S MOTHER: Hi, Kate. How are you?

KELLI'S MOTHER: Well, I am afraid I have some difficult news to share with you. This is a hard call for me to make because I am feeling very embarrassed and ashamed about something Kelli has done, but I need to be honest with you so that we can work together to make the situation right.

CLASSMATE'S MOTHER: Okay. Thanks for calling. I'm getting nervous here. . . .

KELLI'S MOTHER: I want to start off with an apology on behalf of my daughter. This morning, I was looking at her Instagram account and discovered that she posted a photo that featured your daughter's rear end. Several kids, including Kelli, posted some very unkind comments about the photo. As soon as I saw the photo, I immediately had Kelli remove it from the site, close down her entire account, and delete the photo from her phone. I am mortified that she took the photo in the first place and shocked that she posted it online, because she and I have talked about this kind of thing and she knows that this violates all of our family's values and rules. I am so sorry to tell you about the situation, but I know that you have the right to know about it. I want Kelli to be able to make amends to your daughter and to your family.

The targeted teen's mother could respond to Kate in any number of ways. She could reply with shock that her daughter has been victimized, with anger over the cruelty, with uncertainty over what Instagram even is, or with confusion over how the situation will impact her daughter. She could threaten immediate legal action or downplay the seriousness of the event altogether. Best-case scenario: She would thank Kate for her candor in bringing the incident to her attention and arrive quickly at a problem-solving frame of mind. Realistically, a rational, solution-focused response might take some time to achieve, following a predictable and natural rush of emotions about the revelation.

Truth be told, Kate has no control over how the classmate's parent will respond. She only has the power to manage her own words, tone, and attitude. In this case, Kate has chosen to be upfront, apologetic, and proactive in dealing with her daughter's actions directly, rather than downplaying them or sweeping the cyberbullying under the rug. Adults who approach kids' mistakes and misbehaviors in this way put themselves in the best position to teach young people better ways to behave in the future.

You may be wondering about Kelli's role in taking responsibility for her actions. Should she have been the one to call the targeted girl's parents? In some situations, it is entirely appropriate for the child to initiate the contact and indeed, this situation does call for Kelli to apologize directly to her peer. Still, there remains a place for adults to interact with other adults when it comes to issues like this one that have potentially far-reaching and long-lasting consequences for kids. Yes, there are some instances of online aggression that kids can handle entirely on their own, but no, adults should never assume that young people have the skills to do so without the benefit of adult guidance, role modeling, and instruction.

Conversation With the Personal Friend Whose Daughter Also Participated in the Cyberbullying

KATE: Hi, Tina. It's Kate.

TINA: Hi, Kate. How are you?

KATE: Not so great. I actually have some difficult news to share with you. I discovered something that Kelli and Emma have been involved in that I am really upset about. I am calling because I want to make sure that you are aware of it too so that you can do whatever you need to do on your end with Emma.

TINA: Is this about the Instagram thing? Emma just told me about it. She said Kelli texted her and said that she got in a lot of trouble with you for posting a photo. I saw it and honestly, it didn't seem that bad to me. That girl needs to wear pants that aren't so tight or she should expect the other kids to talk about her, don't you think?

KATE: Um. Well. No, actually, I would disagree with that. I feel really shocked that Kelli would take a picture like that and even worse that she would choose to post it for others to see. We have rules about what she can and cannot do online and this was a clear violation of all that we have talked about. I feel horrible for the girl. She must be humiliated!

TINA: Emma says the girl doesn't even know about it. I say we should keep it that way. The photo is off of Kelli's page. No harm done.

KATE: I'm sorry, Tina, but I disagree. I think a lot of harm has been done to the girl. Honestly, even though the photo is not on Kelli's page anymore, the image is still out there with other kids' mean comments. I was calling you to let you know in case you wanted to address the situation with Emma. I already had a conversation with the girl's mother about the photo, so the girl is aware of what is going on. I can't just sweep something like this under the rug.

TINA: Well, I have to say that I think you overreacted to this whole thing, Kate. Kids will be kids. It's the world they are living in. They share everything online now. We can't take it all so seriously. We just have to let them deal with it.

KATE: Okay. I understand your point of view on this. I guess we'll have to agree to disagree. I am very upset with Kelli for her part in this and I don't think this is part of everyday life for her or any of the kids. A photo like that is beyond kid stuff or everyday fun. It was meant purely to embarrass the girl and I am not going to let Kelli think that it's okay to be cruel like this.

It's not uncommon for even close personal friends to differ widely on their approach to cyberbullying. Part of what makes this form of aggression so confounding is the lack of agreement among adults on how seriously to take it or how to handle it with their kids.

As in the first dialogue scenario, Kate cannot control how Tina will respond to the situation or how she will choose to discipline Emma. She can only make decisions about how she will approach Kelli and the standards she will set for her own family. At the very least, by making her standards clear, Kate will have the power to impact the behavior of her own daughter. At best, her honest and assertive response will provide a model for the seriousness with which her parenting peers will consider the issue of cyberbullying. Change often happens slowly, but it begins person to person, parent to child, and peer to peer.

Educate Kids About Netiquette and Acceptable Online Behavior

When the Internet first became a powerful force, the term "netiquette" was coined to describe ethical ways to interact while online. Though no equivalent phrase has yet emerged for cell phone use (cell-iquette?), it is important for professionals and parents to establish a set of standards for how kids must behave while using technology and to educate young people about the rewards and risks of interacting with peers via technology. As with most aspects of working and living with kids, there isn't a simple one-age-fits-all formula for the safe use of technology. The eight rules below offer adults a set of universal principles to share with kids. The rules speak directly to young people and offer practical guidelines on how to use technology in ways that respect the dignity of their peers and reflect the positive values of most schools, organizations, and families:

1. **Choose your words carefully.** If you wouldn't say something to a person's face, don't send it via text or the Internet. Technology

makes it too easy to say things that are impulsive or unkind. Also, the person reading your message can't see your facial expressions or hear your tone of voice. Sarcasm and humor often get lost in translation on the 'Net, so avoid their use. Type carefully as well; avoid using ALL CAPS since they make it look like you are angry or YELLING.

2. **The Internet is not a weapon.** Don't gossip about other people while you are online. Your words can be misinterpreted, manipulated, and forwarded without your permission. Plus, it's not fair to talk about people when they can't defend themselves. Likewise, social media sites should never be used to strategically exclude peers who are on the outside of a peer group or to unfriend a person after a fight.

3. **What you post is permanent.** Once you share something online, you lose control of where it goes, who can forward it, who will see it, and how it can potentially be used. As much as you might believe right now that you can trust your boyfriend with intimate photos or your best friend with secrets, you should still refrain from sending either of them any personal information online. You can't imagine it now, but someday, that information could be distorted and used against you.

4. **Who is this message for?** What happens in cyberspace stays in cyberspace—forever. Though you may intend to send your private message or photo to a single recipient, keep in mind that it can be cut, pasted, and forwarded to an infinite number of people. Never post a photo or message that you wouldn't want everyone to be able to view.

   While on the subject, be thoughtful about the photos and videos that you allow your peers to take of you. Sometimes, these images start off as fun but can be used in embarrassing ways later on. Always have all of your clothes on and don't engage in any kind of joking behavior on film that can be taken out of context or used against you later on.

5. **WWMT?** Be kind and do not ever use e-mail to say ugly, nasty, or mean things about anyone or to anyone. Stop and ask yourself, "What would Mom think if she read this?" Post accordingly.

6. **Take it slowly.** In this world of instant messaging and constant contact, you may be tempted to say whatever comes to your mind in a given moment. Don't give in to the temptation. Slow down and think before you post whatever thought, comeback, or reaction is on your mind—especially if you are feeling an intense emotion like anger or sadness. Wait until you have had a chance to think things through and cool your head before you post a message that can't be taken back.

7. **Don't talk to strangers.** Remember that message your parents gave you when you were little? It still applies today and is very important to remember when you are online. Predators lurk in cyberspace and have clever, hidden ways of soliciting personal information from young people. Never share private information online, including your full name, home address, personal photos, school name, or phone number.

8. **Understand the law.** Cyberbullying is against the law. Now you know. Claiming that you don't is not an option. In fact, ignorance of the law is not a viable defense for any young person and those caught using technology and social media to intentionally inflict emotional distress on others may be punishable by fines and even imprisonment. That "harmless" photo that your friend posted online? It humiliated its subject; she is experiencing real pain. The friend who posted it is legally liable. So is anyone who forwards it. The joking harsh comment you wrote? Now, you are legally responsible as well.

Monitor What Kids Are Doing Online

In response to a conversation about cyberbullying recently, I heard someone bluster, "I don't know what the big deal is—all of those sites and gadgets have parental controls on them. Parents should just use them and be done with it."

If only it were that simple. I agree with the speaker's basic advice about activating parental controls: Adults should use them. However, I caution all parents not to rely on them as a sole means of safety for kids. Parental controls are limited—and we all know

---

Exercise: Encourage Kids to Teach Each Other

One of the best ways to educate young people about the rewards and risks of technology is by encouraging them to share helpful information with each other—after all, kids are the true experts when it comes to online interactions.

If you are working in a school or group setting, have kids develop and present cyberbullying prevention tips and strategies to students in lower grades. Encourage kids to use technology to teach about technology. For example, kids may create and share an antibullying video message with their peers via YouTube. Or they may develop a brief PowerPoint presentation to teach classmates about cyberbullying. Both projects give young people the opportunity to use technology in constructive ways and to engage audience members directly with the subject matter.

At home, ask an older sibling to write three to five realistic scenarios about cyberbullying for a younger siblings. Challenge kids to work together to develop realistic, effective responses to each situation. In this activity, parents gain knowledge of the typical cyberbullying situations their kids are encountering and siblings get the opportunity to work together toward positive solutions. As needed, parents can provide guidance.

---

how good kids can be at testing limits. Automated safety features are a great first line of defense—best fortified by discussion, guidelines, standards, knowledge, interest, effective monitoring, and a whole lot of support for kids.

What does effective monitoring of kids' online activities look like? It varies by age, for sure. Young children benefit from—and really enjoy—an adult's active participation (read: sitting at their side) in their online explorations. In the preschool and early elementary school years, kids don't need protection from cyberbullying as much as they need a foundation in how to navigate between

Web sites, work with apps, protect their online identities, and avoid unsafe people on predatory Web sites.

As kids age, the monitoring becomes both trickier and stickier. By the upper elementary school years—and certainly by middle and high school—kids have the knowledge, ability, and drive to use technology independently of adults. They may even own their own smartphones or have computers in their bedrooms, which makes adult monitoring all the more difficult. Prevention is certainly worth a pound of cure when it comes to keeping kids safe online, which is why it is so important that prior to kids' independent use of technology, adults have done a good job establishing connections with them and educating them about acceptable online behavior. From there, do adults hold their breath and hope for the best? Well, yes, but there are also many other effective things professionals and parents can do.

Know a Child's Passwords

When the time comes to allow a child access to a cell phone, Twitter, Skype, Chatroulette, YouTube, or any other piece of today's ever-evolving technology, adults are not overstepping their bounds to maintain the right to access a child's accounts at any time. Be alert, however: As online activity evolves, more and more social networking sites don't even require individual accounts or passwords, but rather allow for open, anonymous, come-and-attack-as-you-please access. A study by MediaBadger cited 4Chan, an image-based bulletin board that allows anyone to post comments and share images without any preregistration or account creation, as the top mode of online bullying for boys (Crouch, 2013).

The freedom offered by technology can tempt even the most trustworthy, responsible kids to engage in risky behavior, so it is important for adults to let kids know upfront that they will be reading texts, reviewing MMS messages, scrutinizing Facebook posts, viewing YouTube uploads, and providing any other kind of oversight that underscores the importance of safe technology usage. Yes, older kids will always learn new ways to thwart "intrusions" on their privacy, but still, it is always the adult's role to establish values, standards, limits, and accountability.

An important distinction to draw for kids: sharing their passwords with trustworthy adults is important, but giving their passwords to friends is downright dangerous. Trusted friend one day, sworn enemy the next; when kids give up their passwords, they are giving up control of their personal accounts, their online identity, and potentially their good reputation.

Parents, if your child is using a social networking site such as Facebook, ask to friend him or her or, at minimum, ask another trusted adult to do so. While a kid may initially resist this as spying, when parents present this guideline as coming from a place of love and concern for the child's well-being, the young person's sense of paranoia often melts away.

Set Up Parental Controls and Alerts

As noted above, parental controls are an important first line of defense in monitoring kids' online activities, although they should never be considered foolproof or sufficient in their own right. Parental controls can be activated free on many devices or purchased via Internet security companies. They offer many important features, including these:

- Monitoring of all Web sites visited on a specific device
- Recording e-mail, Webmail, instant messages, chats, and social networking activity
- Blocking undesired Web sites and users
- Blocking online advertising, malware, phishing, and so on
- Taking screenshots

Google Alerts provide an effective way for adults to monitor the online activities of a particular child. A parent can set up a Google Alert to notify him by e-mail each time a child's name, username, tagged image, e-mail address, or other identifying information is mentioned on the Internet. Google Alerts can be readily customized and help adults stay up to date with what is being said, shared, and posted by, for, or about a particular child at any given time.

Put Computers in Common Areas

Whether in a school classroom, a youth lounge, or in the family home, computers are best placed in common areas where all adults can easily pass by and see what is going on. Even the best, brightest, and kindest of kids can get caught up in the temptation to do something mean, watch something in poor taste, or stand by idly while a peer is victimized. Putting a computer in a common area will not stop this behavior entirely, but it will make young people think twice about who is watching their activity and whether or not they should be engaging in it. Having kids think twice about online behavior is precisely the adult's goal.

Keep Conversations Going

Discussions about the safe use of technology should not be regarded as a once-and-done item to check off of a to-do list. Rather, adults should maintain an ongoing and open dialogue with kids about what they are doing, what they are seeing, and how they are behaving online. Since most kids tune out very quickly at the hint of an adult-initiated lecture, asking questions is an ideal way to facilitate this communication:

- Would you say the words you are texting to a person's face?
- What would your parents think if they read this e-mail?
- Could this message you are sending cause hurt or embarrassment to you, your friends, your family, or anyone else?
- What do you like about this video? What makes your friends want to watch and share it?
- Can your text be taken out of context?
- What kinds of things do your friends share on social media?
- If you received a threatening or rumor-spreading text message, what would you do?
- How does technology make it easier for you to say something unkind to someone?

Cell phones and social networking sites are prime tools of bullying among young people, so consistently reiterating the message that texts, phone calls, and social media sites are never to be used as tools of gossip, exclusion, or embarrassment is essential.

Include Cyberbullying in School Policy

Most state laws on bullying include specific provisions about cyberbullying. Schools and other youth-serving organizations should likewise set clear, written guidelines for the safe use of technology among young people. These policies should include a mechanism for the safe reporting of cyberbullying and protocols for what happens when students violate established rules. Cyberbullying policies should be clearly communicated to both students and parents. Many schools require kids to sign antibullying pledges, which can be helpful in documenting that policies have been discussed and agreed upon.

Hirsch and Lowen (2012) suggest that schools go a step farther and designate a point person that is responsible for keeping up with current laws related to cyberbullying and being knowledgeable about best practices in stopping it. This on-site cyberbullying expert would be the liaison with parents as well as with local law enforcement.

Put It in Writing at Home

For parents and caregivers, a simple way to ensure that you have clearly communicated guidelines to kids about their use of technology—and to confirm that they have received your message—is to use a technology contract. The most effective contracts are those that parents develop with their kids through conversations, exchanges of ideas, and mutual agreement. That's not to say that young people should get to make their own rules when it comes to using technology, but it is to point out that when kids feel they have a say in establishing standards, they are typically more invested in maintaining them.

Technology contracts should be simple, straightforward, and comprehensive. They are best when grounded in specific values, such as dignity and respect. Contracts marked by a punitive series of "Thou shalt nots" tend to speak less to kids' hearts and therefore inspire less of a commitment to uphold their standards.

Professionals and parents can find templates for cell phone, e-mail, and social media contracts online. These examples are often a great place to begin a conversation about technology safety. Parents and kids can then work together to customize contracts based on specifics for each young person's age and stage. At the outset of the conversation, it is useful to assure kids that the purpose of the contract is not to limit their freedom, but rather to give them a clear framework for enjoying the rewards of technology within the structure of their family's values.

Last, a word of caution to adults who do choose to use technology safety contracts with kids. Keep in mind that these documents can be highly useful tools for opening up dialogue about online behavior and maintaining discussions about important values. They are not, however, to be confused with actual legal documents. A contract with a child works best when it is revisited often. On the other hand, adults who make the mistake of putting a signed contract on a shelf and thinking its impact will endure without ongoing discussion might as well consider that agreement with the child null and void.

Give Technology a Rest

One of the biggest threats that technology poses to young people is the opportunity for constant connectivity. Kids feel compelled to check what other people are saying to them and about them at all hours of the day—and well into the wee hours of the night. Have kids give technology a rest. Schools and youth leaders can establish reasonable rules about the use of cell phones and technology during the day. Parents can set standards for putting technology to bed at night—safely nestled in chargers, away from

Exercise: OMG! How Well Do You Know the Cyberlingo?

Texting has a language all of its own. Laugh out loud (LOL), just kidding (JK), and be right back (BRB) are common enough, but while most adults that are parents today take for granted that ATM stands for a bank's automated teller machine, kids can tell you that it is more likely to refer to being at the mall.

Much of online lingo is cryptic, clever, and intentionally elusive. The over-30 crowd may never know all of the acronyms, but the more professionals and parents educate themselves about the terms their kids are using, the better able they are to monitor technology use and abuse.

How Well Do You Know (DYK) the Cyberlingo?

(Answers can be found on the next page.)

1. BFF
2. TTYL
3. ROTFLMAO
4. CICYHW
5. CYE
6. FYEO
7. FWB
8. 420
9. 53X
10. LMIRL
11. AITR
12. MOS
13. Code 9
14. TAW
15. IMGC

As you review the "translation" of each commonplace acronym, found on the next page, take a moment to tune in to your personal thoughts and feelings about each one. What thoughts come to your mind as you consider specific terms young people use to communicate with one another? How does it make you feel to become aware of the type of content they exchange? What do you make of the lengths kids go to to disguise their communication from supervising adults? How can you become a helpful presence in this covert world?

Just when think you have these terms figured out, kids' cyber-lingo will evolve and change. The challenge for professionals and parents is to stay current. At any given point in time, adults can research common lingo just by typing "Texting acronyms" into an online search engine. But beware: Many of the terms that come up will be profane. This is the reality of the online world. Our kids know the language; adults need to know it too if we want to stand a chance of guiding young people safely through their cyber-worlds.

DYK the Cyberlingo? Quiz Answers

1. BFF: Best friend forever
2. TTYL: Talk to you later
3. ROTFLMAO: Rolling on the floor laughing my ass off
4. CICYHW: Can I copy your homework?
5. CYE: Check your e-mail
6. FYEO: For your eyes only
7. FWB: Friends with benefits
8. 420: Marijuana
9. 53X: Sex
10. LMIRL: Let's meet in real life
11. AITR: Adults in the room
12. MOS: Mother over shoulder
13. Code 9: Parents are around
14. TAW: Teachers are watching
15. IMGC: I might get caught

---

bedrooms. If you wouldn't let your child roam outside late at night without supervision, why allow him unfettered access to technology at all hours? One involves physical safety; the other involves emotional safety; and both are vital to a child's healthy development and well-being.

Make Access to Technology a Privilege

It is important to remind kids that their use of technology and social media is a privilege. Parents should make it clear that this privilege can be restricted or revoked at any time, in any way, if the established rules are violated.

Hold Kids Accountable for Their Online Behavior

In a study of middle and high school students, researchers asked kids what would stop them from bullying other kids online (Kraft and Wang, 2009). Kids cited parental discipline in the form of taking away their access to social networking sites as the top deterrent, followed by parents taking away their computers or phones. It is important that kids are aware of potential consequences of their poor online behaviors at home, in school, and according to state law, and that adults follow through on holding kids accountable in meaningful, compelling ways.

Is forbidding access to technology altogether the answer? Some adults ponder this question very seriously, reasoning that when they were kids, they survived without social media sites or texting—and their kids can too. It is true that many current professionals and parents spent their formative years in an era in which interactions were not dominated by technology, but the reality is that adults have to raise kids in today's world—not in the world from a generation ago. At home, at school, at work, and beyond: Young people are going to have access to technology. Far more helpful than banning digital activity altogether is teaching kids how to manage it safely, with respect for themselves and others at all times.

Communicate Rules in the Context of Caring

No matter how sophisticated kids become in their knowledge of technology, they are still kids. Adults do young people a service by bearing this fact in mind and remaining vigilant in guiding them.

Monitoring by adults need not be done in a suspicious, distrustful way, but rather the efforts adults make to keep kids safe online can be communicated as acts of caring and concern. "I am doing this because I love you," I remind my own daughters. "OMG!" I can hear them think.

Technology Safety Strategies: What Kids Can Do

In this key, I have talked at length about what professionals and parents can do to keep young people safe in their use of technology. Perhaps the most important role of adults, however, is to empower kids to be their own first line of defense when it comes to preventing and ending cyberbullying. Adults and kids share in common the need to keep interventions simple in order for them to be useful. What follows are eight guidelines that kids of any age can easily understand and activate in their personal lives.

1. Reach Out to an Adult

The rules of responding to cyberbullying are not much different from the guidelines for handling other types of bullying. In both cases, it is critical that young people reach out to trustworthy adults to let them know about instances of online aggression. Adults can do a lot to make cyberbullying situations better—but they can't do anything if they do not know about them.

2. Disengage

A young person's instinct in a cyberbullying incident may be to strike back against an aggressor—to return the insults, post equally lewd photos, or spread retaliatory rumors. Never do it. Two wrongs don't make a right, but vengeance can lead to three bad outcomes:

- It ups the ante on aggression. The person who started it will likely escalate the cruelty even further.

- It creates equal culpability in the eyes of adults. Accountability is not based on who started it but rather on who did the right thing to bring the situation to an end.
- It can potentially land both kids in legal jeopardy, since cyberbullying can be a criminal offense.

This is not to say that the recipient or observer of cyberbullying should simply ignore the aggression. There are many powerful actions kids can take (refer to the rest of the rules presented here) but revenge is often the worst choice.

3. Log Off and Block Harassers

Adults spend a lot of time teaching kids skills for making friends, but less effort is put into reassuring kids that in certain instances, it is important to walk away from toxic friendships. Young people should know that a first line of defense in stopping cyberbullying is logging off from an account temporarily. Unlike a face-to-face interaction that is sometimes more difficult or awkward to get away from, kids have the ability to instantly end a digital conversation. They should be encouraged to do so the minute they recognize that cruelty has begun. If they later question their own instincts about whether a particular interaction was really so bad, they can always initiate contact again when cooler heads prevail. In the moment, it is best to disengage completely and log out for safety's sake.

In cases where the harassment is repeated, young people should block the aggressor altogether. Blocking is a powerful, assertive statement of strength that a young person can use to let others know that she will not allow herself to be mistreated.

4. Use Privacy Settings

In regular life, we call them boundaries. Online, we call them privacy settings. Kids should be educated and empowered to use them. In a world where a young person's self-esteem is often measured by a number (e.g., of Twitter followers, of Facebook friends, of Instagram likes, of simultaneous text conversations), kids may balk at pruning their own field, but it is an empowering thing to remind young people that they are in charge of how they are treated by others, rather than the other way around.

5. Take Screen Shots

While reports of cyberbullying are believable, accusations are also deniable. Kids should be taught to take screen shots of incidents of cyberbullying, including offensive e-mails, texts, Facebook posts, Tweets, photos, phone numbers, and so forth. This kind of solid evidence, when shared with adults, can go a long way in bringing cyberbullying to a screeching halt.

6. Step In to Stop It

Kids should be aware that even if they are not the originator of a cruel online message, when they forward it, like it, or even see it without doing something to stop it, they become part of the problem. In Key 6, we will talk extensively about the role bystanders can play in stopping bullying. The important note here is that young people never forward, share, or passively condone cyberbullying activities.

7. Empathize

As they prepare to post any message via technology, young people should bear in mind one thing: There is a human being on the receiving end of their keystrokes. Too often, technology numbs kids to the reality that their words can wound others. That depersonalization explains why young people say things online that they would never say to someone's face. One of the most basic things that kids can do to stop cyberbullying is to remember that their message is going to a person, not just to a device.

8. Take Personal Responsibility

Along with the depersonalization of a recipient's feelings, young people sometimes lose track of the fact that their actions in the virtual world have consequences in the real world. Young people will make mistakes online. Adults should encourage them to own up to their poor judgment and make genuine amends to anyone they have hurt via technology. Acknowledgment and accountability are both strong deterrents to repeated online aggression.

Exercise: Cyberbullying Prevention Action Plan

What standards do you set for young people when it comes to technology usage and netiquette? How do your accountability standards for behavior online compare to your standards for kids' actions offline?

Create a cyberbullying prevention action plan for your work and life with kids. Include specific guidelines, technology contracts, privacy setting standards, accountability protocols, and discussion starters that will be useful in helping your young person use technology in safe, dignified ways.

---

10 Practical Strategies to Deal Directly With Cyberbullying

1. Encourage young people to have as much face-to-face interaction with their peers as possible.
2. Foster positive connections with young people that encourage open dialogue about high-risk situations like cyberbullying.
3. Be open to learning about less-than-desirable online activities of your own child and be assertive enough to reach out to other parents to keep them informed about otherwise hidden online activities of their kids.
4. Teach good digital citizenship. Talk with kids directly about acceptable and unacceptable uses of social media and technology.

5. Use technology contracts as a springboard for dialogue about online activities and cyberbullying.

6. Teach kids about the permanency and replicable nature of online posts. Foster discussions about the Internet's almost-infinite audience.

7. Learn and stay up to date with kids' cyberlingo.

8. Include very clear standards about cyberbullying in the school's bullying policy.

9. Carefully consider policies for cell phone usage in schools and at home.

10. Directly address and report any unethical online behavior by young people.

KEY 5

BUILD SOCIAL AND
EMOTIONAL COMPETENCE

Recently on Facebook, a national organization that provides mental health services for school-aged children posted an open question for followers: You witness a student being bullied; what do you do?

Hundreds of people responded within the hour. The majority of answers were focused squarely on punishing the aggressor—most with a vitriol and a vocabulary that would shock the very children they felt so strongly about protecting. "Shame the bully!" responded one teacher, who boasted that her 22 years of classroom experience validated her answer. "Kick the kid out of school," demanded another.

Ouch.

As much as Facebook is a reliable barometer of public opinion, it is clear that a pervasive knee-jerk reaction to the problem of bullying is flat-out hostility. The response is understandable: Adults who were victimized by aggressive kids during their own youth often feel a strong urge to protect the current generation of young people from the same kind of abuse. Likewise, many adults feel justice is best served when aggressors are punished for their wrongdoing.

Yet the problem with antibullying strategies that center on the behavior of the bully is that they leave targeted kids in a powerless position, assuming that their lives will get better only if the child who bullies changes his or her ways. In fact, in their landmark study, Davis and Nixon (2010) found that adult actions aimed at changing the behavior of children who bully are actually more likely to make things worse for their victims—not better.

Bullying prevention programs that shift their focus to building social and emotional competencies in all kids achieve better results. Studies by the Collaborative for Academic, Social, and Emotional Learning (CASEL, 2011) clearly show that effective SEL programming drives important social outcomes such as positive peer relationships, higher levels of caring and empathy, increased social engagement, and reduction in problem behaviors such as bullying. What's more, students who receive SEL programming academically outperform their peers and graduate at higher rates. For schools driven by standardized test scores, this approach to education cannot be ignored.

In this key, we begin by examining which kids benefit from gaining social and emotional competence and hear what kids have to say when questioned about which SEL skills actually make bullying situations better. We will look in depth at the five content areas most frequently cited as vital parts of any bullying prevention approach in schools. Because the peer group is such a vital force in young people's lives, we will pay special attention to the skills that help kids establish and maintain positive friendships. As throughout this book, what you won't find in this key are complicated, multistep programs to implement; what you will find are practical, engaging, easy-to-use ideas for fortifying kids to cope with bullying.

Who Benefits From Social and Emotional Learning Programming?

A 5-year-old girl can't figure out how to tie her shoelaces into a proper knot. Her mother demonstrates the skill and waits patiently while the child practices the process over and over (and over!) again. The activity takes a lot of repetition on the part of the child and is aided by abundant affirmation from the parent. Then finally—voila! The child gets it and demonstrates mastery over the skill. Within days, she is sharing her knowledge with others, including helping her best friend learn to tie her shoelaces.

In school, an eighth grader struggles in algebra. Quadratic equations just don't make sense to him. He is frustrated and feels inadequate. His teacher sits at his side and reviews the formula for solving the equation, breaking it down into step-by-step terms that the child is better able to comprehend. A lightbulb goes off in the teen's head and for the first time in years, he starts to feel competent in math again.

A young person bullies a fellow student. He is caught. He is punished. He is sent back to class.

The contrast is stark and it is clear; when kids lack a basic life skill or struggle with an academic concept, adults approach them from a teaching framework, but when young people demonstrate social deficiencies, adults too often simply punish. To change the culture of bullying in our schools, communities, and families, we must alter the way we approach the development of social and emotional competencies, moving beyond a punitive framework and forward to a system that teaches kids specific skills for navigating social dynamics and managing interpersonal conflict.

Do all kids need these skills? Why not separate out the instruction for just the kids who bully or for young people known to be particularly vulnerable to bullying? Any child can benefit from SEL skills because, as author Carrie Goldman (2012) points out in *Bullied*, getting through life requires all people to manage social dynamics. Indeed, human beings are called upon to use social skills every day of their lives, at all ages, throughout the life span. It only makes sense for formal education, whose goal it is to develop productive citizens, to provide explicit instruction in these skills.

Further, when talking about effective bullying prevention approaches, we are not focusing narrowly on the behavior of just a few, hand-selected kids, but rather aiming to make schools and communities healthier places for all who dwell there. Studies demonstrate that SEL programming is an effective way to reduce the likelihood of bullying among all young people because it promotes skills, behaviors, attitudes, and environmental factors that are incompatible with bullying (CASEL, 2011).

At What Age Should SEL Programming Be Implemented?

The early school years are a critical window of time in the social and emotional development of kids. Parents, teachers, counselors, and other trustworthy adults are still highly influential at this age and in an ideal position to shape a young person's thoughts, feelings, and behaviors when it comes to bullying (Anthony & Lindert, 2010). If bullying behaviors peak during the middle school years, it stands to reason that unwanted aggression takes root during elementary school. SEL programming, then, should be implemented from the earliest school years to meet this need.

Further, according to Social Thinking founder Michelle Garcia Winner (2013), middle schoolers are the most resistant learners because they believe adults have little to offer them. When kids are young enough to still believe that the adults in their lives have valuable information to impart when it comes to socialization, we must seize the opportunity to teach them well.

On a related note, young people throughout the school years do some of their very best learning within small groups. While kids with more significant social disabilities may require one-on-one intervention by adults, most school-aged kids learn social skills best within a group setting because this affords them the unique opportunity to simultaneously learn new skills, practice them on their same-age peers, and receive immediate feedback. Kids provide a mirror for one another that is qualitatively different than the type of reflection adults alone can offer them. What's more, authentic and compassionate peer feedback instills confidence in young people that what adults are teaching them in terms of social skills has real-world value.

What Skills Do Kids Say They Need to Manage Bullying?

As professionals and parents, we like to believe that we know what is best for kids. In their groundbreaking study, researchers Stan Davis and Charisse Nixon set out to discover if we are right. Through the Youth Voice Research Project, Davis and Nixon (2010) interviewed over 12,000 students in elementary, middle, and high schools, across diverse gender, race, and ethnicity lines, all across the United States, asking young people about the strategies and skills they believe they need to cope with bullying. Their goal was to compile a body of knowledge describing the most helpful interventions for reducing bullying in schools.

The results of the study are revealing and invaluable in informing SEL programming at all levels. When asked "Which strategies made things better?" young people cited the following strategies most often:

1. Told an adult at home.
2. Told an adult at school.
3. Made a joke about it.
4. Told a friend.
5. Hit them or fought them.

When asked "Which strategies made things worse?" the strategies most frequently cited by kids included:

1. Hit them or fought back.
2. Made plans to get back at them.
3. Told the person to stop.
4. Did nothing (ignored it).
5. Told the person how I felt.

Interestingly, "Hit them or fought back" appears on both lists. It seems likely that this physically aggressive response makes victims feel empowered in the moment and may even gain them peer attention, but has long-term costs in terms of conflict escalation, increased fear of retaliation, and punitive consequences at the hands of schools, parents, and even the law.

A significant finding in the analysis of the youths interviewed is that kids were most likely to identify actions that accessed support from others as the ones that made the most positive difference in dealing with bullying. In contrast, strategies aimed at changing the behavior of kids who bully tended to make things worse for their targets. For professionals and parents working to design and utilize SEL skills to help kids cope with bullying, these findings—straight from the mouths of students—are compelling.

Five Components of a Bullying Prevention SEL Program

As noted in Key 1, most schools now have policies that guide their practices on bullying. While these policies are vital to have in place, a truth that most professionals, parents, and kids can verify is that policies don't change people; people change people. Young people who struggle with social interactions don't develop new skills because a policy told them they ought to and kids who like to dominate and control others don't give up these behaviors because they read a rule on a poster. On the other hand, CASEL (2011) studies confirm that students engaged in SEL activities show higher levels of prosocial behavior, exhibit lower levels of conduct problems and emotional distress, have more favorable attitudes toward school and their peers, and achieve more academically. Bottom line: SEL programming fosters the educational and social conditions that make bullying far less likely.

Since bullying is social in nature, it's important to have a bullying prevention program that focuses on increasing kids' social and emotional competence. The Committee for Children (2013) cites five content areas that are vital parts of any bullying prevention SEL program. In this section, I define and describe each component with a practical emphasis on specific activities and skills that adults can teach kids. Fortunately, SEL programming is rich in resources for professionals and parents. Readers can easily access scores of SEL curricula, designed and customized for a wide range of kids' needs, through professional catalogs, mass-market bookstores, and even online. The activities described in the sections below are offered as an immediate sample of the types of programs available to kids and selected because of their applicability across a wide range of kids' ages and stages. Readers should note that the activities described below provide a framework for thoughtful discussion with kids and are most effective when customized for individual or small-group needs.

1. Emotion Management

All kids have feelings. Some kids are had by their feelings. It is not uncommon, in fact, for young people to become so overpowered by intense feelings of anger, sadness, fear, or frustration that their whole bodies respond. We have all seen it: the red face, the tears, the shaking, the balled-up fists, the yelling, the aggression. Learning to manage strong feelings in constructive ways is a process for young people. For some, it takes longer—and requires more explicit instruction—than others.

In this area, SEL programming focuses on increasing kids' self-awareness and teaching them to recognize personal triggers for intense emotions early on, before they become overwhelming. Kids who bully and kids who are bullied alike need skills for managing stress and controlling their impulses. Emotion management programming also helps kids learn techniques for self-soothing. In this skill area, kids are encouraged to reach out to helping adults to communicate their feelings in constructive ways rather than lashing out aggressively at others.

Bullying Prevention Ideas for Kids

- **Create a "bug list."** Include all of the things that tend to bug you and make you feel frustrated, angry, sad, or scared. Share this list with a teacher, parent, or even a classmate. Describe how you usually respond to each item on the bug list. Is this response helpful or hurtful? With a partner (a classmate, teacher, sibling, or parent) brainstorm more constructive ways that you can use to respond to things that bug you.

- **How do you chillax?** Most kids can easily name the things that make them feel upset, but many find it challenging to know how to chill out after a stressful situation. How do you relax after a fight with a friend? What makes you feel calm after reading a mean post on Facebook or finding out that your friends all went to a party without you? It's natural to get riled up in a conflict and to want to strike back at people who have hurt you, but this is never a good idea; reacting in anger almost always makes situations worse. Make a plan for yourself about how you will chill, relax, and thoroughly calm down after a stressful incident, before you respond to it. Share the plan with a parent and ask him or her to help you stick to it—every time. Cooler heads always prevail in a conflict.

- **Reach out.** One of the worst parts about a conflict with a friend is that you feel like you are all alone. In the moment, you may feel like there is no one you can talk to and nobody who would understand what you are going through. It may be true that your situation is unique and yes, you may even have gotten yourself in pretty deep, but the truth is, you are never alone. It is helpful to identify key people that you will go to in times of trouble before the trouble begins, so that when your mind plays tricks on you and you feel isolated, you don't have to think so hard about who to talk to or where to turn. Can you talk to a parent? A neighbor? A counselor at school? Sometimes reaching out to a person who lives far away is helpful—a relative can listen to your situation objectively and support you without making you feel judged or pressured to follow specific advice. More often than you would ever imagine, when you reach out and confide your experiences to others, you'll discover that they have experienced similar feelings and can understand just where you are coming from.

2. Empathy

Empathy is the ability to walk a mile in someone else's shoes—to understand how another person is thinking and feeling in a particular situation. In the world of bullying prevention, empathy is an important skill to develop in young people because kids who bully often get caught up in the social rewards they receive from their behavior (e.g., a sense of power and control over others, increased peer attention, greater social status) and lose touch with the hurtful impact their aggression has on their victims. SEL programming focused on empathy development plays a preventative role in bullying because it teaches kids to feel for each other in very human ways, rather than to view peers as pawns in a popularity game. Effective empathy development activities guide young people to be consistently mindful of how others are thinking and feeling.

Bullying Prevention Ideas for Kids

One particularly powerful empathy-building activity, simple to deliver and instantly applicable for kids of all ages, is this one, popular around the Internet and generally attributed to a wise but unnamed educator:

- A teacher in New York was teaching her class about bullying and gave them an exercise to perform. She had the children take a piece of paper and told them to crumple it up, stomp on it, and really mess it up but not to rip it. Next, she had them unfold the paper, smooth it out, and look at how scarred and dirty it was. Then, she told them to apologize to the paper.

  The teacher pointed out that even though the kids said they were sorry and tried to fix the paper, the scars remained. She explained to her students that those scars would never go away completely, no matter how hard they tried to fix it. "That is what happens," she said, "when a child bullies another child; they may say they're sorry but the scars are there forever."

The looks on the faces of the children in the classroom told her the message hit home.

While the internet version of this activity ends here, an empowering follow up is to challenge kids to brainstorm a list of realistic actions they can take to support a person in the aftermath of a bullying incident. Specific examples of before, during, and after-the-fact interventions for bystanders are provided in Key 6. The message for adults to emphasize is that while words wound—and some scars do endure—a young person's empathic act of kindness and demonstration of support does have the power to heal.

Other effective, engaging, and easy-to-implement empathy-building exercises encourage kids to assume multiple points of view on a single situation.

- For younger kids, develop realistic role-plays in which a child first has to take on the needs and wants of one character and then, without warning, is assigned to switch roles and plead the case of the character he had just been opposing. Follow up with questions that encourage the child to reflect on how she felt playing each role and how the process of switching roles helped her better understand each character's point of view.
- For older kids, learning the skills of debate not only look good on a college application but can also be tremendously useful in teaching kids to look deeply at both sides of a situation. Good SEL programming often integrates academic lessons with social ones.

Last, activities that teach kids skills for effective listening are a key part of empathy development. It is only by learning how to listen to others that kids (and adults) get an accurate window into another human being's worldview.

- **Hearing versus listening:** What's the difference? Even though hearing is one of the basic five senses, actual listening does not come naturally to most people. Begin this activity by engaging kids in a conversation about the differences between the passive act of hearing and the active process of listening. Ask questions such as these:
  * What is the difference between hearing and listening?
  * How do you show, in terms of your behaviors, that you are truly listening to someone?
  * How does it make you feel when you know that a person can hear your words but is not really listening to what you are saying?
  * Can you share an example of a time this occurred? What did you do in the situation? Did you continue to talk? Did you stop talking? Did you say anything to the person about how they made you feel? Why or why not?
  * If you are talking, and someone jumps in right away to share her point of view, do you feel you have been truly listened to? Why or why not?

Allow kids ample time to explore the differences between hearing and listening, then follow up the discussion with this activity:

- Assign kids to work in pairs. Assign the roles of Person A and Person B.
- Tell all of the Person As in the group to spend one full minute telling their partner, Person B, a story. (The story can be about anything—a made-up story or a real-life event. The main point is for Person A to talk for a full minute.)
- In this first round, Person B should be assigned to use poor listening behavior in response to the partner. The adult may offer specific suggestions (e.g., poor eye contact, interrupting, texting on a cell phone) or challenge Person B to come up with his or her own inattentive listening behaviors.
- After the minute is over, lead a discussion about how both Person A and Person B felt during the round. For example:

* What did it feel like to talk to Person B?
* How did you know Person B was not listening to you?
* Did you want to stop talking before the minute was up?
* Did you feel like Person B cared about you?
* How did it make you feel about Person B?
* How did it feel to be so inattentive to Person A?

- Next, assign a second minute of talking. This time, Person B should do the talking, while Person A uses good listening behaviors (e.g., good eye contact, nodding, leaning in).
- Follow up with a discussion about how the good listening behaviors made each person feel.
  * What did it feel like to talk to Person A?
  * What were the behaviors that showed good listening?
  * How did good listening make you feel?
  * How did it make you feel about Person A?
  * How did it feel to be so attentive to Person B?
  * Did listening well help you understand Person B in a new way?
- Conclude the activity with a summary discussion about the positive impact that effective listening has on a relationship with an emphasis on what an active process good listening is. Connect the skill of making a person feel listened to with the skill of empathy and making a person feel understood.

3. Problem Solving and Conflict Resolution

Building a bullying-free culture is not to be confused with having a conflict-free environment. Conflict is a natural part of human interactions and disagreement can be productive when it helps individuals consider all relevant perspectives. A key in bullying prevention SEL programs is to teach kids problem-solving skills that help them manage life's inevitable conflicts in independent and respectful ways. Researchers have found that problem-solving strategies are thirteen times more effective in de-escalating conflicts than aggressive, retaliatory, or emotionally reactive responses (Wilton, Craig, & Pepler, 2000).

Bullying Prevention Ideas for Kids

- **Finding win-win solutions:** Often, conflict situations are resolved according to a winner-takes-all philosophy, in which one child gets all of his needs met while the other loses out completely. This is really more of problem-generating approach, however, as hard feelings usually lead to new conflicts in short order. Give kids practice developing win-win solutions that honor and fulfill the interests, wants, and needs of all parties involved in a conflict. Learning how to compromise is a life skill that helps kids maintain balance as they navigate the choppy waters of social dynamics.

- **Sharing SODAS:** In *Friendship and Other Weapons* (Whitson, 2011a), I outline an easy-to-remember problem-solving strategy for kids. This approach guides kids in systematically defining problem Situations, brainstorming all possible Options for its resolution, determining the Disadvantages and Advantages of each option, and ultimately selecting a Solution for the problem (SODAS). The SODAS method is as easy as it is analytical; its formulaic approach makes young people feel competent to solve problems independently while its built-in evaluation of advantages and disadvantages guides kids in choosing the best possible solutions.

- **Turn a problem into a solution:** Write a letter to a person that has bullied you. In this letter, do not focus on the ways in which the other person has hurt you, but rather tell him how his actions have motivated you. For example, if the bully was a former friend who stopped talking to you, tell him how his behavior prompted you to explore a new activity, join a different team, and look for positive friendships in new places. Or if a person used to threaten you or physically assault you, tell him how you have now learned ways to defend yourself and stand up for others at the same time. Once you have written the letter, keep it in a very special place. It is not meant to be sent, since the letter really has nothing to do with the person who bullied you. The letter is all about you—a tribute to your strength, your resilience, your unstoppable spirit, and your ability to turn any problem situation into an opportunity.

4. Assertiveness

Assertiveness is a style of communication in which a person expresses his or her thoughts and feelings in a verbal, nonblaming, respectful way (Long, Long, & Whitson, 2009). Whereas the aggression that characterizes bullying is destructive to relationships because it aims to hurt or depreciate others, assertiveness builds positive relationships though its honest and respectful approach. When kids learn and practice assertiveness skills, they become better able to communicate clearly, negotiate conflict independently, resist peer pressure, fulfill their own needs, and connect effectively with peers and adults.

Bullying Prevention Ideas for Kids

Passive, Aggressive, and Assertive Styles
In the context of bullying prevention, assertive communication is the essential middle ground between aggressive comebacks that escalate hostilities and passive responses that reveal a longing for approval and lack of power. The more a child who bullies realizes he can pick on a victim without a direct response, the more he will do it. Using the example below, challenge kids to consider which response would be most effective in neutralizing the power of a child who bullies:

ABBY: Where'd you get your outfit—the clearance rack?

RESPONSE 1: Yeah, my mom made me wear it. I love what you have on, though. You always look so awesome.

RESPONSE 2: I got it out of your closet, bitch.

RESPONSE 3: Knock it off, Abby.

For discussion:

- **Response 1:** Passive. The first response feeds the bully just what she wants—power. By complimenting Abby after such an obvious put-down, the target hands herself over, saying, "Reject me again, hurt me some more. Whatever you say is okay because I am just so desperate to be liked."
- **Response 2:** Aggressive. The second response challenges Abby

to escalate her aggression. Snappy, humiliating comebacks invite bullies to keep the conflict going and turn up the heat for the next round.

- **Response 3:** Assertive. The third response is assertive, letting Abby know that the victim does not intend to be victimized. It does not seek forgiveness, but does not pose a challenge either. It is simple and unemotional.

Why should kids be taught to use responses that are unemotional? Kids who bully tend to be excellent psychologists and pick up on subtle cues that a potential target can be emotionally impacted. This vulnerability signals the aggressor that he will be able to wield power easily. By teaching young people assertiveness skills that project confidence rather than anger or fear, kids who bully detect less potential for wielding control.

A Bit More on Effective Comebacks

When I was a child—and often still to this day—I thought of my best comebacks 10 minutes after the situation in which I really needed them. Unfortunately for people who share my plight, the phrase "better late than never" definitely does not apply when talking about comebacks. Truly, the only thing worse than a bad comeback is a good comeback delivered with bad timing. For that reason, it is very helpful for adults to teach kids effective phrases to use during teasing situations before the situations actually occur.

Psychologist Liz Laugeson (2013) says that the way in which kids respond to teasing determines both how often and how severely they tend to be teased in the future. She explains that a common behavior of kids who are naturally socially accepted is that in teasing situations, they act like what a teaser says doesn't bother them. To do this, the socially savvy kids tend to give brief, disinterested, bland responses to the teasing, including phrases such as these:

- Whatever.
- Tell me when you get to the funny part.

- Seriously?
- Your point is?

Helping adults can work with kids individually or in groups to brainstorm a list of verbal comebacks, in addition to the ones above, that effectively drain all of the fun out of teasing and decrease the likelihood that a child will be the target of teasing again in the future. After a list has been compiled, use role-play to allow the child(ren) the opportunity to practice saying different nonchalant phrases aloud and observing others' reactions as they strategically feign indifference. The more kids have the opportunity to think through and practice various comebacks aloud, the better prepared they will be to use them on the spot during a teasing or bullying incident. In the next section, we talk about how to pair assertive body language with effective comebacks.

Don't Mix Signals

An important component of assertiveness training is teaching kids to use body language that reinforces their words. Use role-play to teach kids these simple, nonverbal strategies for showing the world that they mean what they say:

- **Use a calm, even tone of voice.** Shouting, cursing, or using a shaky voice negates the power of assertive words.
- **Maintain an appropriate distance.** Stand well within earshot, but not in the bully's face or shrinking back.
- **Use the other person's name when addressing her.** This is an assertive technique that lets an aggressor know she is your equal.
- **Look a person directly in the eye.** Maintaining eye contact is a mark of emotionally honest and direct communication.

5. Friendship Building

For school-aged children, friendships create a powerful sense of belonging. A vital component of SEL programming, especially in the context of bullying prevention, is helping young people develop skills for both making friends and choosing positive friend-ships. In this section, we explore these related but distinct skills.

Making Friends

For many young people, the ability to make friends comes as natu-rally as breathing, but for others, connecting with peers is utterly confounding. As noted in Key 1, for example, kids on the autism spectrum often find it particularly difficult to join social groups, leaving them isolated and vulnerable to bullying. We know that chronic peer rejection robs kids of important opportunities to in-teract successfully with their peers and, in doing so, to develop the kinds of healthy social skills that lead to social support. Bullied children, then, find themselves in a vicious cycle of rejection, so-cial avoidance, and isolation.

Focused SEL programming can be very effective in teaching young kids who struggle socially to adopt prosocial behaviors. At the same time, it is important to keep in mind that good SEL programming is not limited to kids who are bullied, nor it is about teaching kids to "act normally" so that they won't be victimized. Rather, effective SEL curricula are comprehensive, reach out to all students, and focus broadly on helping kids of all abilities man-age social dynamics.

Choosing Positive Friendships

Sometimes social skill deficits have nothing to do with why a par-ticular child becomes the target of relentless bullying. In *Odd Girl Out*, Rachel Simmons (2011) points out that bullying is very often context specific and has more to do with the dynamics of a par-ticular peer group than with any personal characteristics of the identified target. For example, a young person who finds herself consistently victimized in her school classroom may find herself valued and accepted by her basketball teammates—or vice versa.

Help Kids Cast a Wide Net

It is not at all rare for schools to be unfriendly territory for kids to find and form close relationships. The competition for rank on the

---

Exercise: What Skills Does Your Child Need?

Kids who struggle socially need specific adult guidance in developing the skills to reach out to their peers and establish friendships. Think about a child you know who has difficulty making friends. Make a list of the child's strengths:

- Is he particularly interested in a certain subject—animals or science or technology?
- Does she enjoy a particular activity—swinging or swimming or listening to music?

What are the particular challenges this young person has in connecting with others?

Based upon your consideration of this child's unique strengths and challenges, what are the social skills he would benefit from adopting? Identify the child's top two or three needs, then think about how these skills can be infused into a classroom curriculum or daily interactions with the child.

Now think about a child who is socially astute and displays a tendency to dominate peer interactions. This child may choose bullying as a way to fulfill his drive for power and control. Frame his desire to be in control as a strength; call it leadership. What social skills can you teach this child to harness his strengths and channel them into works of empathy, compassion, and positive leadership?

---

school social ladder can be intense and many otherwise kind kids choose to bully their peers as a way to rise in the local social hierarchy. In these kinds of school cultures, it's a kill-or-be-killed mentality. One of the simplest, yet most powerful things that adults can do for kids who are caught in this kind of environment is to provide out-of-school opportunities for kids to form positive relationships with similar-aged peers. Both professionals and parents can play a

vital role in encouraging kids to cast a wide net, seeking out friendships in their neighborhood, on a team, through a club, with a
youth group, or in the arts. In doing so, adults expose kids to multiple peer groups and all kinds of friendships. When a child does
connect with a positive peer, the adult plays a critical role in holding that friendship up to the light.

Teach Kids to Know What to Look for in a Friend
Along with teaching kids where to look for positive friendships,
adults offer kids a lifelong skill when they teach them what positive
friendships should feel like. In their younger years, kids tend to be
intuitive in their friendship choices; they make decisions on whom
to play with based on fundamentals such as who likes the same
games and toys, and who is kind to them. As kids age, however,
social dynamics become more complicated and motivations for
seeking friendships change. It is not uncommon for upper elementary and middle school students to choose friendships based on
social status alone.

The logic goes something like this: "She is popular, so if I can
become her friend, I will be popular too."

Or the corollary: "She is not considered cool. I like her, but if
I spend time with her, people will think I'm a dork, so I'm not
going to talk to her anymore."

There is even a tolerance for toxic friendships that sounds like
this: "She is really mean to me. She insults me and always makes
fun of me in front of our friends, but if I don't hang out with her,
I won't have anyone to hang out with, so I'll just put up with the
way she treats me."

It's a sad fact of the tween and teen years that kids lose touch
with their childhood instincts that gained them their first real
friendships. For many, it takes years to regain the self-confidence
to choose friends based on the qualities of the person rather than
the person's social status. Adults can play a role, however, in influ-
encing kids' choices when it comes to friendships and limiting the
toxicity of their friendships.

SEL has everything to do with facilitating situations in which kids feel accepted and embraced by their peers. In experiencing these moments, kids relearn what real friendships should feel like. Professionals and parents can facilitate this insightful process by engaging kids in dialogue about what to look for in a real friendship.

Bullying Prevention Idea for Kids

Around the dinner table at home, during downtime at school, or in the car (always a great place to have a conversation with a young person), turn the discussion into a finish-the-sentence game with a starter like, "I know someone is my friend when she . . ." Hopefully, the end of the young person's sentence will sound something like this:

- Is kind to me
- Takes turns
- Shares
- Tells me how she is feeling in words
- Listens to what I have to say
- Laughs with me (not at me)
- Helps me
- Makes sure that I am included
- Is comfortable with me having other friends
- Is there for me when I need her
- Cares about what I say and how I feel
- Encourages me and makes me feel good about myself
- Stands up for me
- Is fun to be with
- Has a lot in common with me

The items on the list will vary by age, of course, but the values of what a healthy friendship should look and feel like are consistent at most ages. When adults take time to provide specific instruction for young people on choosing friendships with these qualities, they equip kids to enjoy strong social support and to extricate themselves from toxic, hurtful peer relationships.

What Do You Do When a Child Clings to a Frenemy?

In kids' earliest years, parents spend hours arranging playdates and planning parties. Professionals pair kids up to work together and monitor their partnerships. Adults are careful architects (some call them "cruise directors") of kids' positive social development. Then the day comes when a child makes—and tenaciously maintains—a toxic friendship. Then what?

The once überconfident, joyful child is now anxiously and obsessively trying to please a friend who wields power by being unpleasant. When that inevitable day comes that a child's best friend starts acting more like a frenemy, what should you do? Should you do anything? Before moving on, take some time to consider how you will know when the time is right to intervene in a child's friendship struggles and what you will do or say to help her navigate the dynamics.

Ending a Toxic Friendship

Professionals and parents do not have to look far to find SEL curricula designed to give kids skills to make friends. Bookstores and online sites provide at-your-fingertips ideas for fun ways to teach kids prosocial behaviors. Many of these strategies can be very effective when implemented consistently by a nurturing adult. What is more difficult to find, on the other hand, is helpful instruction for young people on how to end toxic friendships. It's hard enough for young people to accept the realization that a friend has turned into a frenemy, but to disengage from that friendship without causing an avalanche of drama can feel impossible to kids. In this real-life situation, a high school student confided her friendship struggles to a school counselor. The counselor, in turn, gave her a few pointers on how to end a toxic friendship with dignity:

STUDENT: I invited Nikki to my graduation party. From the minute she got there, she started making fun of everyone and everything. She told me that one of the other girls I invited was a loser and that I had better be careful or people would start thinking that I was a loser too. She said my graduation dress was "hideous." When I explained to her that my mother had made it by hand and that I didn't like it much either but felt like I had to wear it, she started telling everyone that I was too poor to buy clothing. She was bossing me around and when I wouldn't do what she told me to do, she started texting another friend of ours, telling her how lame my party was.

I put up with it for a long time, but finally I told her that the way she was acting was not cool and I wanted her to either stop it or leave. She just laughed and said, "You're being so sensitive today. Can't you take a joke?" When I saw her in school on Monday, she acted like nothing had even happened. This is not the first time something like this has happened either. Nikki treats me like this all of the time. I don't know what to do but I don't want to be friends with a person who treats me like this.

COUNSELOR: It never feels good to be let down by another person. We all put so much stock in our friendships and in how good it feels to belong that sometimes it can be really hard to realize when a friend is no longer good for us. It took real maturity on your part to even acknowledge that you don't like the way Nikki is disrespecting you and a lot of courage for you to talk to me about it. I am proud of you.

STUDENT: Thanks. I thought you were going to tell me to go back to class and handle it on my own. I guess this is all just really stupid.

COUNSELOR: Feelings are real. They are not stupid and you don't ever have to handle them on your own. What would be foolish would be trying to ignore them or act like they don't matter. It's important that you always surround yourself with people who take your feelings seriously—whether it is me, another staff member at school, your parents, or even . . . yes . . . your friends. You tried to tell Nikki how you felt about the way she was treating you at your party and she told you that you were being too sensitive. In other words, she didn't take your feelings seriously. It's okay for you to want more from a friend. It's a healthy thing for you to move away from people who disrespect you.

STUDENT: I am totally not talking to her anymore!

COUNSELOR: What I want you to keep in mind is that the way you go about moving away from Nikki is important and will say everything about the type of person you are. Create distance with dignity. Don't get into ugly wars of words with her, then half apologize by saying you were "just joking"; that will only bring you down to her level. Also, resist the urge to talk badly about her to other friends—in person, online, by text, or in any way, shape, or form. In fact, don't put much of your energy on her at all. Shift your focus to what is going right in your life—to the friendships and activities that make you feel good about yourself. Think about what you are doing and who you are with when you are your best self, then plan your day accordingly. It might not be smooth sailing the whole way through, but if you keep it classy on your end, you'll free yourself up to find better friendships and know that there is life after Nikki.

The counselor listened, took the student seriously, and validated the student's maturity. She affirmed the young person's right to be treated respectfully and gave her practical advice for moving away from the friendship with dignity. Often, by the time students like this one come to adults, they have an inkling of what they need to do but are uncertain of how to go about doing it or lack the confidence to move forward with their instincts. Adult validation of kids' constructive intuitions is key. In this case, the counselor gave the student permission to move on from the toxic friendship and guidance in doing so gracefully.

Keep It Steady: Do Not Speak Ill of Friends or Frenemies

Last on the subject of friendships, it is important to discourage kids from disparaging a friend with whom they are "on the outs," just as the counselor did in the situation with Nikki. Kids' friendships are constantly re-aligning. When kids say negative things about each other during a short-term conflict, they can create long-term damage. Likewise, when adults contribute to negative conversations about kids, they may find themselves on the outside of the circle of trust when the child makes up with the friend. To be most effective, adults need to stay in the position where the young person is talking with them openly.

How Much Time Should Be Dedicated to SEL Programming for Kids?

In school cultures dominated by the pressure to achieve high test scores and in daily lives rushed by the race to complete never-ending task lists, the question of how much time can be dedicated to teaching kids social and emotional competencies is an important one. The answer is less clear-cut, however. Surely, a paragraph in a book fails to convey the intensity of the effort, patience, repetition, and time that it takes to teach any new skill to a child. Just as we wouldn't expect young learners to master cursive writing in a class period or memorize math facts in a day (or even in an entire school year, for that matter), nor should we expect something as abstract and complex as social skills to be mastered in a single group lesson or brief school-wide assembly.

Learning how to master human interactions is a lifelong process and one that deserves to be taught to kids over a period of time. The good news is that SEL does not have to stand alone and take significant time away from other mandated academic lessons; rather, as we have noted, good SEL programming can be easily infused into regular classroom lessons. Rather than rushing SEL programming or giving up on it when new skills don't take hold quickly, helping adults are wise to be patient, to be persistent, and to forgive kids if they bungle many a peer interaction along the way.

Last Word on the Subject

Despite the intense pressure in public education for students to perform well on standardized tests, there is no research evidence indicating that test scores lead to better overall outcomes for kids in adulthood. There is abundant evidence, on the other hand, that having good social skills results in positive outcomes for young people during their school years and throughout their lives (Winner, 2013). Integrating SEL into standard school curricula, from the earliest years through high school graduation, is a proven way to fortify kids with the skills they need to cope with bullying and to thrive in all of their interpersonal interactions.

*   *   *

SEL Resources for Children, Tweens, and Teens

One of my favorite ways to connect with young people is through books. While adult-child conversations can quickly morph into one-way lectures, lessons woven into stories have great potential to reach and teach young people in engaging, enduring ways. The following books, roughly listed in order from youngest readers to older ones, are just a handful of my favorites (see the Resources section in the back of the book for more).

For elementary school-aged kids, it is a wonderful gift to be able to read books aloud to individual students or to small groups of kids—even chapter book readers in the upper elementary grades still often enjoy a good read with a grown-up. For middle and high school readers, professionals can assign books as part of a reading list and initiate one-on-one or group discussions of the books, as necessary. Parents can share resources with kids, (re)reading books alongside their sons and daughters and initiating nonthreatening dialogue to process kids' thoughts, feelings, and general responses to each one.

No matter which books are selected or how they are used, the key is to keep conversations enjoyable. The point of using books (aside from the fun of a good story) is that fiction is often less threatening than fact. Rest assured: Allowing kids to talk about bullying concepts in relation to a story, without feeling the urgent need to drill down to how the story relates to personal experiences, is enough.

Jungle Bullies by Steven Kroll

Jungle Bullies is a picture book for preschoolers that uses rhyme and repetition to share important messages about standing up for yourself and learning to share. With engaging, child-friendly illustrations and inviting jungle animal characters, this is a great choice for introducing concepts about friendship and bullying to the youngest readers.

Bullies Never Win by Margery Cuyler

This easy-to-relate-to children's book tells the tale of Brenda Bailey, a bully who persistently and relentlessly taunts and teases her classmate, Jessica. Cuyler creates an accurate portrayal of how targets like Jessica typically respond to bullying, including experiencing anxiety, losing sleep, quitting sports, changing their style of dress, and fearing asking for help. She also uses Jessica to show young readers that the best way to handle bullies is to stand up to them in assertive ways.

The Bully Blockers Club by Teresa Bateman

The Bully Blockers Club harnesses the power of the group in standing up to—and stopping (err, make that "blocking")—bullies. In this cute story for preschool and early elementary school readers, Grant Grizzly teases Lottie Raccoon mercilessly, withstanding all of her best individual efforts to ignore him and walk away. But when Lottie rallies others kids who have been bullied by Grant into a club designed to stop the Grizzly in his taunting tracks, they find strength in numbers and success in standing up for one another.

The Recess Queen by Alexis O'Neill

I love the power of a well-written rhyme and this story has it—and so much more. When I saw this title on a bookstore shelf, I quickly assumed it would be a tale about relational aggression. Mean Jean the Recess Queen does not use friendship as her weapon of choice, however. Rather, she dominates the playground with obvious, outward physical aggression, "swooshing, pushing, and lollapalooshing" the other kids. What makes the tale even less stereotypical (and even more effective) is the way in which the Recess Queen is disarmed by the least likely of her peers. *The Recess Queen* is a good story for young readers about the power of kindness and friendship in transforming relationships.

Confessions of a Former Bully by Trudy Ludwig

Since we're on the subject of confessions, here's mine: Trudy Ludwig is one of my all-time favorite children's book authors. Her messages are so entirely genuine and relatable that kids can't help but connect with the characters in her stories. *Confessions of a Former Bully* is written as the diary of "Katie," a young girl who undergoes a transformation from bully to former bully, taking readers along on her journey. It is a visual delight of a book, using engaging illustrations and eye-catching text boxes to highlight meaningful messages, memorable facts, and helpful phrases that young people can use during encounters with kids who bully.

My Secret Bully by Trudy Ludwig

My Secret Bully, written for tween readers, lifts the lid off the hidden culture of relational aggression, otherwise known as girl bullying. It tells the story of Monica and Katie—two girls who have been friends since kindergarten, but who now are facing a rift in their relationship, as Katie begins to exclude and embarrass her former friend in front of their other classmates. In tackling this painful subject of the ways in which some girls use relationships as weapons, Ludwig provides an accurate and not-often-addressed portrait of a young girl's anguish at the hands of a frenemy. *My Secret Bully* is not a lighthearted portrayal of bullying, nor does it offer pat answers. But it does address an important issue in the lives of upper elementary and middle school–aged girls and can serve as a great springboard for discussions with parents.

One by Kathryn Otoshi

You know how sometimes a book comes along that you just know you will hold onto long after your child is done with it? Borrowing it from the library will not do—you have to own it and you are certain it will be a top gift pick for any of your mom friends. For me, that book is this one. Part of the magic of *One* is the significance of its message, conveyed in the simplest of terms and illustrations. This multiple award winner is one of the best books I've read on the subject of the power that one child can have to change a bullying situation and to stand up for herself in a way that garners self-respect and promotes dignity for all.

Stand Up for Yourself and Your Friends:
Dealing With Bullies and Bossiness, and
Finding a Better Way by Patti Kelley Criswell

This book is part of a collection of resources written for tweens by American Girl. *Stand Up for Yourself and Your Friends* is not a story, but rather an easy-to-read collection of strategies, tips, and suggestions for how girls can effectively cope with bullying. Using fun quizzes and advice from real kids, this book feels like a teen magazine but will last longer and can be referred to time and again.

Wonder by R. J. Palacio

August Pullman was born with a serious facial deformity that left him unable to attend regular school for the first several years of his life. When he started fifth grade at Beecher Prep, he hoped to be treated like any other kid but first had to navigate his classmates' wonder—and sometimes disgust—at his outward appearance. *Wonder* lightens the heavy topic with humor and takes tween and teen readers on a really unforgettable path of empathy, compassion, and acceptance.

Story of a Girl by Sara Zarr

This book takes a jump ahead of the others in terms of age-appropriate content, but it is an important resource to have on the list, given how prevalent the issue of slut shaming is for tweens and teens. In this true-to-life fictional account, 13-year-old Deanna Lambert's life is forever altered after she is caught in the backseat of a car with her older brother's best friend. This book can be a springboard for important conversations about actions, repercussions, reputations, resilience, and redemption.

SEL Resources for Professionals and Parents

These days, professionals and parents have a myriad of resources available to help them reach out to young people and teach them critical skills for coping with bullying. The trick is to zero in on activities and lessons that are a good match for a particular child, student, class, or group. Truth be told, there is no single right program; rather, a sincere and committed adult makes all of the difference in how to customize lesson plans and present new material to engage young hearts and minds. The following list offers some of the SEL programs and curricula that I believe to be most effective.

A word to the wise: The best SEL lessons are not always so great the first time they are delivered. If you read an activity and it strikes you as a powerful message for kids, be willing to try it more than once. Sometimes it takes a bit of repetition for you, as the adult, to get your words, rhythm, and presentation style just so. Be willing to work out kinks and stick with effective messages—the kids are worth the effort and the lifelong skills you will ultimately impart are worth every second of your time.

Friendship and Other Weapons: Group Activities to Help Young Girls Aged 5–11 to Cope With Bullying, by Signe Whitson
In recommending this book (in no particular order, of course), I share with readers my 12-session SEL curriculum that uses thought-provoking discussions, engaging games, strength-discovering exercises, and confidence-boosting fun, to build critical knowledge

about relational aggression and teach friendship survival skills to young girls. *Friendship and Other Weapons* offer users easy, step-by-step guidelines for each session and photocopiable resources to use with kids (www.signewhitson.com).

The Bullying Workbook for Teens: Activities to Help You Deal With Social Aggression and Cyberbullying, by Raychelle Cassada Lohmann and Julia V. Taylor

Per its name, *The Bullying Workbook for Teens* is designed for young people to use independently, as a self-help resource for learning tips and strategies to cope with bullying. As such, it is a very valuable resource, but because I believe that kids learn best in the context of supportive relationships, I recommend that professionals and parents become familiar with this book as well, and use it to guide kids in their development of specific emotional and behavioral skills.

Bully Busters: A Teacher's Manual for Helping Bullies, Victims, and Bystanders, by Dawn Newman-Carlson, Arthur M. Horne, Christi L. Bartolomucci, and Dawn A. Newman

This program is organized into seven modules, each of which offers educators specific topical information and provides multiple classroom activity options for helping kids cope with bullying. The Bully Busters program is distinctive for its encouragement of teachers, students, and parents to work together to stop bullying (http://www.bully-buster.com).

Steps to Respect

From the Committee for Children, Steps to Respect is a comprehensive school-wide program that provides both guidance for adults (administrators, teachers, cafeteria workers, and bus drivers alike) on their role in bullying prevention and classroom lessons for kids on how to recognize, respond effectively, and report bullying. The Steps to Respect programs are designed for kids in kindergarten through sixth grade (www.cfchildren.org).

The Olweus Bullying Prevention Program, by Dan Olweus
Founded in Norway, OBPP is among the most researched and the
best-known bullying prevention programs in the world. Useful for
students in elementary, middle, and high school, it has been shown
to result in up to 70% reductions in bullying, victimization, and
antisocial behavior among kids. OBPP is designed to improve the
social climate of classrooms and promote positive social relationships among students (www.violencepreventionworks.org).

The Peaceful School Bus Program: A Program
for Grades K–12 by Jim Dillon
Knowing that bullying often occurs in the places and spaces where
adult supervision is limited, the Peaceful School Bus Program is
designed to create a climate of respect and cooperation and decrease inappropriate behavior on school buses. Not limited to just
bus behavior, however, this whole-school program (for elementary,
middle, and high school students) uses team-building games and
mentoring programs to comprehensively stop bullying behaviors
(www.peacefulschoolbus.com).

PACER's National Bullying Prevention Center
This is a program of the PACER Center (Parent Advocacy Coali-
tion for Educational Rights), an organization that seeks to enhance
the quality of life of children and young adults with disabilities.
PACER Center activities are based on the concept of parents helping parents. Their National Bullying Prevention Center offers tool-
kits and activity ideas for parents, teachers, and other professionals
to use with young people of all ages (www.pacer.org).

10 Practical Strategies to Build Social and Emotional Competence in Kids

1. Make social skills instruction a part of the school-wide curriculum and everyday interactions with kids.

2. When kids show cruel behavior toward one another, approach them from a teaching framework, rather than a punitive one.
3. Give young people the skills they need to treat others with dignity, then hold them accountable for maintaining those standards of conduct.
4. Talk to the students in your school to find out what they find most helpful—and least helpful—when it comes to bringing an end to bullying.
5. Use role-playing to help kids practice using strong body language, assertive phrasing, neutral tones, and other effective communication skills.
6. Engage kids in conversations about what positive friendships should feel like.
7. Fortify young people with the skills they need to cope with the anxiety and sadness caused by bullying.
8. Teach kids that they have choices when it comes to emotional expression. Provide instruction on anger expression styles.
9. Cultivate kids' extracurricular interests to help them develop supportive friendships, experience real joy, and gain social confidence.
10. Be a role model of assertive emotional expression, problem solving, and conflict resolution.

TURN BYSTANDERS INTO BUDDIES

As a therapist in a residential treatment facility very early on in my career, I worked with adolescent boys and girls who came to our program with long histories of truly appalling abuse. By the time these kids were 13, they had lived more life and endured more pain at the hands of others than most people do in their lifetimes. Truly.

Which is why it always threw me for a loop when the events that provoked these kids to the height of their anger or the depth of their despair were slights by peers. One would think—I certainly did—that young people who had been through so much real trauma would be immune to so-called petty drama but, as it turned out, injuries at the hands of their peers were often particularly acute. A single incident that I recall as most searing for one 15-year-old boy occurred one afternoon on the bus on the way home from school:

I recall noting that JP was especially quiet that day when he stepped off the school bus. His normally boisterous demeanor was completely subdued and instead of devouring an afternoon snack as he usually did, he sat silently in a seat in the residential living room, waiting for Transition Time to end. I remember thinking that JP was about to bite a hole through his lip, he was chewing on it so intensely. When I asked him if he wanted to be excused from the group, he practically ran to his room.

I gave him about 5 minutes alone before I knocked on his door to see if he was okay. I half expected to see a room torn apart—clothing balled up or furniture tossed about; it was not unusual for JP to act out his emotions in physically destructive ways. That afternoon, however, I found JP sitting on his neatly made bed, head in hands, tears streaming down his face. He was initially embarrassed that I saw him crying, but motioned for me to stay.

When I asked him what was wrong, he told me plainly that the kids ("kids" was not actually his choice of words, but I'll let you imagine the colorful terms he chose) on the bus were messing with him again, teasing him about not having a girlfriend and calling him "gay." "But the worst part about it," he said before breaking down completely, "was that Keith was sitting right next to me and never said anything to stop them! I thought he was my best friend."

JP was inconsolable for more than 20 minutes after that. I sat with him while he cried. I could tell he needed the release. The remarkable thing was that I had been working with JP for more than 6 months at that point and I had never seen him so much as tear up. This young man with an unfathomable history of loss, abuse, and violence was brought to his knees by the experience of betrayal by a friend. In many ways, it was a milestone in JP's ability to acknowledge and express emotion but treatment breakthroughs aside, I will never forget the impact of Keith's nonbehavior on JP and always remember how tremendously impactful the peer group can be—for better and for worse—in the lives of bullied kids.

The Role of the Bystander

Research suggests that peers are present during nine out of every 10 incidents of bullying but intervene on behalf of victims less than 20% of the time (Hawkins, Pepler, & Craig, 2001). The same study documents that when peers do step in to stop bullying behaviors, however, the episode stops within 10 seconds, more than half of the time. Imagine the impact bystanders could have on bringing an end to bullying if they intervened at higher rates. It is our job, as adults, to figure out how to get them to do so.

Why Don't Bystanders Intervene?

There has been much research over the years on the "bystander effect" and what makes otherwise good, caring people look the other way when trouble is occurring right in front of them. When it comes to stopping bullying, there are a number of frequently cited reasons that kids tend not to intervene on behalf of their peers.

Diffusion of Responsibility

The diffusion of responsibility theory says that if a person believes that someone else will intervene to help in a troubling situation, then the person tends not to do so. In schools and other group settings, young people often believe that adults will intervene in a bullying situation, thus freeing them of the responsibility to do so.

The trouble with this theory, of course, is that most bullying behaviors are not acted out in front of adults. As we saw in Key 1, in fact, adults may be unaware of up to 96% of bullying incidents. That's a stark contrast to the evidence cited above noting that kids are present almost 90% of the time that bullying occurs. It is kids' very presence, in fact, that often makes bullying so tantalizing to aggressors, as peer attention fuels the young person's sense of power and often raises his or her social status.

Kids, then, must be encouraged not to look to others to intervene but to understand that stopping bullying is their personal responsibility. In the sections below, we will talk about realistic ways that kids can take on this daunting task.

Fear of Becoming the Next Target

One of the most common reasons kids don't intervene in incidents of bullying is because they are afraid that doing the right thing for someone else will be the wrong thing for their own well-being. As in the children's game King of the Hill, kids who bully often push down anyone—and everyone—who threatens their top position. As Barbara Coloroso (2008) points out in her book *The Bully, the Bullied, and the Bystander,* young people are keenly aware that kids who bully are quick to disparage and malign anyone who tries to intervene.

Torn Between Friends

Often enough it happens that a young person witnesses an incident of bullying at the hands of a good friend and while she knows in her gut that what is occurring is wrong, she feels torn about what to do. In her head, she justifies it: "I don't like what she is doing, but she is still my friend." The child then makes the decision not to intervene based on this prevailing desire not to defy a friend. In the world of young girls, the pressure to avoid conflict with friends can be especially intense (Simmons, 2010). Helping kids find ways to surmount this pressure and assert themselves in all relationships is another key role of helping adults.

No Existing Friendship With the Victim

Sometimes bystanders know with certainty that the bullying they are witnessing is wrong, but they rationalize that the person being bullied is not their friend or that they barely know the victim, so therefore it is not their place to defend him or her. This private logic is related to the diffusion of responsibility theory—the bystander believes that someone who is friends with the bullied child will likely step in, so he or she is excused from doing so.

Feelings of Helplessness

In the first key, we noted that oftentimes adults feel helpless when it comes to intervening in a bullying situation. They believe they lack the knowledge and skills to make bullying stop. This is all the more true for young people. To a greater extent than ever before, kids are getting the message in school, from parents, and via media outlets that bullying is wrong, but specific instruction on how to intervene effectively is not always as available.

What to say to stop bullying is an important component of bullying prevention education for adults and kids alike. In Key 3, we talked about concise wording that adults can use to intervene on the spot in bullying episodes. Later in this key, we talk about age-appropriate assertive phrasing that kids can use to stop bullying whenever they witness it.

Exercise: What Kept You From Intervening?

Most of us have been in a situation in which we witnessed wrongdoing but did not intervene to stop it. Think about a time in your life when this was true for you:

- Why did you hesitate to step forward?
- If you could go back in time and live the experience over again, would you behave differently?
- What would you do to intervene on behalf of the person being victimized?

This is an important exercise for adults, as it offers the opportunity to step into the shoes of young people and recall how intimidating it can be for them to make the leap from bystander to ally.

The Negative Emotions Associated With Being a Bystander to Bullying

All told, kids who observe bullying experience a myriad of unpleasant and conflicting emotions: relief that they are not the target of the bullying mixed with guilt over not doing anything to stop it; pity for the person being victimized, tempered by fear of confronting a friend; anger that no one else is intervening blended with confusion over what they could say or do to make the situation better.

What if, instead of these feelings, kids could be helped to feel powerful in the face of bullying? How might their intervention rates increase—and episodes of bullying be brought to a quick end—if young people believed that their actions would have a significant impact and positive outcome?

Making bystanders feel empowered enough to become allies to vulnerable peers is a key component to bringing an end to bullying and the focus of the remainder of this key.

Turning Bystanders Into Allies

To empower young people to intercede on behalf of bullied peers, professionals and parents must first help kids overcome the barriers to intervention, described above. Key focus areas include making sure that all kids:

1. Believe that stopping bullying starts with them: that it is their job to intervene, not someone else's responsibility.
2. Feel a connection with the bullied child. Whether or not they are friends, the bystander must feel empathy for the victim and believe that the victim does not deserve to be mistreated.
3. Understand that conflict is a part of life. While kids may be uncomfortable with challenging a friend's bullying behavior, they must also be confident that the friendship can withstand the confrontation.
4. Know how to use assertive communication to stop bullying whenever they see bullying.
5. Feel confident that their intervention will have a positive impact on the bullied child and have minimal (or at least manageable) negative consequences for themselves.

Exercise: What Can You Do to Help a Child Overcome the Barriers to Intervention?

Consider each of the barriers to intervention listed above. Think of at least two creative ways that you can help a child overcome the barrier. Write these strategies down and make a plan to implement them.

For example, to dispel the diffusion of responsibility theory, host a school-wide contest, challenging each student to create an original slogan that explains his or her role in stopping bullying. Encourage kids to be as creative as possible, displaying their slogans on poster boards, wearing them on T-shirts, or even putting them to music.

This is an activity I frequently use when giving bullying prevention presentations to young students. The creativity it inspires can be amazing. A slogan I use to get kids going is, "It is never okay to do nothing about bullying." Over the years, kids have generated wonderful ideas that demonstrate their understanding of the concept that they own the responsibility to stop bullying. Some of the best slogans kids have created include these:

- Stopping Bullying Starts With Me
- It Only Takes One
- Want a Friend? Be a Friend. Help a Friend.
- Step In. Stop Bullying.
- Break the Code of Silence: Speak Out Against Bullying
- There Is No Such Thing as an Innocent Bystander

How Does Neuroscience Support Empowering Bystanders?

Recent advances in neuroscience offer a compelling argument for why empowering bystanders to become allies is so effective. The key is in two neurotransmitters: dopamine and serotonin. Dopamine is a neurotransmitter that plays a role in several brain functions including reward, behavior, mood, and learning. Studies show that kids who bully may experience a boost of dopamine when they act out against their peers. The dopamine rush activates the reward centers of the brain and makes these kids feel powerful.

As helping adults, we want kids to feel powerful. Confidence and self-efficacy are important lifelong traits to cultivate in all young people. But we want kids to gain these feelings through good works and acts of kindness, not because they have dominated, ridiculed, or manipulated others. The good news is that dopamine is available to the brains of all kids—not just those who bully. When bystanders intervene to stop bullying, they experience their own dopamine rush, as they take control of troubling social dynamics and stop unwanted aggression in its tracks.

Serotonin is the second brain chemical implicated in the cause of empowering bystanders. Sometimes dubbed "the happy hormone," serotonin helps to lift mood, ease tension, relieve depression, and create a general sense of well-being. Studies show that the brain produces serotonin every time a person commits an act of kindness. When bystanders intervene on behalf of a targeted peer, their behavior is reinforced naturally through the brain's surge of this feel-good chemical.

Neuroscience gives us a compelling picture of what the brain finds rewarding. Professionals and parents just need to ask the right questions of bystanders: What skills do you need to be able to step in to stop bullying?

On-the-Spot Interventions for Bystanders

As noted above, research shows that when a bystander intervenes to stop bullying, the unwanted aggression usually stops within 10 seconds. This holds true regardless of the specific words the bystander uses. In other words, it's not how a young person intervenes so much as simply the fact that she does intervene that brings about the desired change (Goldman, 2012). Educating kids that their voice can make a difference is an empowering message with implications far beyond bullying prevention. What a gift for young people to know that their words truly matter.

In the heightened stress of a bullying episode, however, most kids lose some ability to access the thinking part of their brains. They may fight aggressively, freeze in fear, or engage in flight behaviors to avoid the situation altogether, but few have the presence of mind to come up with their best assertive responses on the spot. That's why helping kids develop brief scripts to use during an episode of bullying—long before the episode ever occurs—is so important. In the heat of a bullying moment, a prepared child will not have to struggle to think of what to say, but rather will have effective responses on the tip of his tongue.

A SEL exercise described in my book *Friendship and Other Weapons* is helping kids develop and practice Bully Bans, which are defined as short, to-the-point statements used to stop bullying behavior (Whitson, 2011a). Examples of effective Bully Bans for bystanders may include:

- "Don't say that. That's mean."
- "Knock it off."
- "Not cool."
- "You're taking it too far. Stop."

The message to reiterate to kids is the same one I share with the readers of this book: Intervening to bring an end to bullying does not have to be complex, time-consuming, or premeditated. The most powerful interventions are often the simplest ones—the brief statements, the consistent use of kindness, and the everyday courage to stop bullying whenever you see it.

Before- and After-the-Fact Interventions for Bystanders

One of the main themes of bystander empowerment is teaching kids that there is power in stepping in right away. Professionals and parents do kids a great service by making them aware that there can also be tremendous power in reaching out to bullied kids before bullying has even occurred as well as after an episode of bullying has played out. The key during both time frames is offering peer support and companionship.

Before Bullying

Because of its repetitive nature, bullying episodes can often be anticipated by socially aware kids. For example, a student may be able to predict with a good degree of certainty that a vulnerable peer who is often bullied on the bus ride home will face a difficult drive during a class field trip to a historical landmark that is 25 miles from the school. Young people can learn proactive skills to reach out to vulnerable kids before bullying is likely to occur, by taking such actions as offering to sit with the vulnerable child on the bus ride or alerting an attentive adult to take on a similar preventative role.

In Key 1, we looked at the real-life example of Riley, the girl who was bullied by Jada and Liza on the playground but accused as the aggressor by adults when she responded with impulsive physical aggression. In the aftermath of that situation, it became clear that most of Riley, Jada, and Liza's classmates were aware of the bullying that was taking place, but none of them chose to intervene. When questioned about their decision not to do something to stop the relational aggression during any of the four days leading up to the scarf-pulling incident, the classmates all claimed various versions of the reasons listed earlier in this key: they weren't friends with Riley, they thought the playground aides would intervene to stop Jada and Liza, or they didn't know what to do to stop the situation.

After the full circumstances came to light, professionals in the school were able to use the situation as a springboard for teaching kids that whenever they become aware that bullying is being planned, they should take an active role in telling the planners to stop, alerting an adult about what they have heard, and reaching out to the targeted person to help him or her feel protected, connected, and supported. In the case of Riley, an effective bystander intervention before the bullying would have been for a classmate to offer to play with Riley during recess. In that way, Riley would not have been so desperate for Jada and Liza's attention and not as vulnerable to their repeated manipulation.

Exercise: What Skills Would You Encourage?

What skills would you encourage the classmates of Riley, Jada, and Liza to use if they overheard Jada and Liza's planning or observed Riley's daily humiliations on the playground?

After Bullying

While it is not always possible to anticipate or prevent bullying from occurring, there is much that compassionate bystanders can do to ease its pain after the fact. Simply taking the time and making the effort to talk to a bullied child following a painful peer encounter by saying something like, "Don't worry about that girl [boy]. She's [He's] like that to everyone," is a powerful reminder to the targeted child that he or she is supported by others and does not deserve the cruelty. When the bystander-turned-ally follows up this brief intervention with an invitation for the bullied child to join a group of friends for lunch or another upcoming social situation, he or she confirms the message that the bullied child is never alone. Other empowering messages that allies can communicate to bullied kids after an incident of bullying include these:

- I am sorry that that happened to you.
- You did not deserve that.
- I think you should tell Mrs. Smith about what just happened. If you want, I'll go with you.
- Would you mind if I tell Mrs. Smith about what just happened? I can understand you might be worried about telling her, but I think she needs to know.
- I'm here for you. You can always come talk to me when something like that happens.
- Find me at lunch/on the bus/at recess/after school from now on. You can hang out with me and my friends.

Exercise: Bystander Intervention Planning

The following activity can be used by professionals and parents on their own, to think through strategies for empowering bystanders to become allies. Or it can be conducted with kids, challenging them to come up with specific strategies to intervene in bullying.

For each scenario below, list at least three ways that bystanders can effectively intervene. Challenge yourself to come up with ideas that can be used before the bullying occurs, on the spot during an episode of bullying, and after bullying has occurred.

Scenario 1

Jessie is furious with Kris. She thinks Kris has been flirting with her boyfriend. Jessie doesn't want to confront Kris about it because she thinks Kris will just deny it and she worries that saying anything will make her boyfriend angry. Instead, Jessie creates a fake Instagram account for Kris, using all sorts of embarrassing photos. Jessie then rallies other kids to post photos on the page, talking about how they hate Kris and what a loser she is. The page catches on in no time and the whole high school seems to know about it.

How can bystanders intervene to become allies to Kris in this situation?

Scenario 2

Darrell dreads his bus ride home from middle school. Every day, the kids who sit behind him slap him on the back of his head and the kids who sit in front of him turn around to shout profanities. They mock him, asking, "What are you gonna do, cry to your mama?" and threaten to beat him down if he tells anyone at school about what happens on the bus. Darrell tries to get his parents to drive him home from school but they both work and are unable to change their schedules. This situation goes on unchecked for months.

How can bystanders intervene to become allies to Darrell in this situation?

Scenario 3

Chloe and Olivia have been best friends since kindergarten. In third grade, they are put in different classrooms and each makes new friends. All is fine at the beginning of the school year, but in early November, Chloe starts to say things to Olivia like, "You're not my best friend anymore" and "You can't sit with me at lunch. This table is only for my new friends." Olivia is hurt but decides to just focus on the girls in her own class. One day in December, Olivia walks into the school cafeteria and finds that no one is willing to sit with her at lunch. Everywhere she tries to put her tray down, kids parrot the exact same message: "This table is only for cool kids. You're not one of them."

How can bystanders intervene to become allies to Olivia in this situation?

Allies Gone Awry: The We-Hate-Madison Club

Teaching new skills to young kids is often like watching a pendulum swing: Before kids can get to the middle ground where they use the skills with finesse, they often show wilder and less-effective extremes. In this real-life example, a group of girls had recently been learning about bystander interventions in school, so when they witnessed their classmate, Madison, bullying another child on the bus, they thought they knew just what to do. This is the story of how one well-intentioned bystander proudly told her mother of how she and her friends "intervened" to stop bullying:

"Guess what, Mom? Jessica said she is going to be in our *We Hate Madison club.*"

"What did you say, honey?" the girl's mom managed to ask. Stomach drop. Head spin.

The mother had heard her daughter's words perfectly clearly and their implications hit her straight away. Her question was just a way of gathering her thoughts—stalling, if you will. And, of course, hoping that she had heard wrong.

"Jessica said she was going to be in the *We Hate Madison* club," the girl repeated, with no trace of guilt or sense of wrongdoing.

The moment the mother had been dreading had arrived. While many parents anticipate that at some point their child will be involved in bullying, no one expects it to be reported with candor and glee. As often as the mom had thought about how she would deal with a bullying situation, she had always pictured having the conversation in a relaxed moment—one in which she and her daughter could pour a cup of cocoa, snuggle on the sofa, and chat for a good hour about the importance of kindness and the values inherent in real friend-ships. She never planned on the conversation happening just fifteen minutes before the school bus arrived, nor did she think she'd be addressing her daughter as the aggressor.

In the few minutes she had, she told her daughter in clear, plain, simple, no-nonsense terms that having a "We Hate Anyone" club was bullying and that it was not okay. Then she told her daughter that she was to have no part of a club like that—ever.

Her daughter looked at her like she was from a different planet. Then she tried to explain: "Oh, no, Mom. It's not like that. Madison is the one that is really mean. That's why we started the club. We saw her stealing her brother's Kit Kat bar on the bus. She is always so mean to him and we are tired of it, so we were just sticking up for him. We all did it at the same time to let her know we wouldn't stand for what she was doing to him."

A small bit of relief flowed over the mother. Her daughter was not completely antisocial. She was not picking on an innocent victim. No, she was part of a vigilante group seeking revenge for a sibling injustice. Terrific.

The mother did take some consolation in learning that the glee in her daughter's voice was not happiness about hurting Madison, but rather her faulty conclusion that if Madison was bullying her brother, then it was okay to be part of a large, organized group that premeditated bad behavior in return. The mom quickly pointed all of this out to her daughter: "If all of the kids on the bus gang up against Madison and create a club around disliking her, that is bullying. It's not okay, no matter what Madison did, to be part of a club like that," she explained.

Before allowing her daughter to get on the bus and face the *We Hate Madison* club crowd again, the mom knew there were two more things she had to tell her daughter—thoughts she needed to let sit with her for the day.

The first was a note about empathy. She validated that Madison's behavior toward her brother sounded pretty mean and told her daughter that it was okay to be upset about it. Then she asked her to consider how it might feel to be Madison and to have all of the kids on the bus against her. She asked her daughter to imagine what it must be like to have a group of people looking at her, whispering around her, but not talking directly to her.

Second, conscious of the fact that thus far she had told her daughter all of the things she could *not* do—like being part of a group whose purpose was to make someone else feel miserable—she knew she needed to tell her what *to* do in the situation. She challenged her to be the hero on the bus—to be the kid who says to the other club members, "Guys, I think what we're doing here is wrong. I know Madison was really mean to her brother before, but now we're being really mean back and I don't think we should do this anymore."

After suggesting these words, the mother got the faraway planet look again. It was clear to her that her daughter was caught totally off guard by the conversation. What the young girl thought was going to be a triumphant moment of heroism on behalf of Madison's little brother turned into a whole different kind of intervention—and she was on the receiving end of it.

It is not at all uncommon for kids to misinterpret social skills instruction or to take new skills to the extreme when practicing them the first few times. This daughter, along with her friends on the bus, thought they were doing the right thing by intervening to stop Madison's mistreatment of her brother. What they failed to understand was how their overzealous response created a new cycle of bullying that was far more vicious than the first one. Adults play an important role not just in empowering bystanders to become allies but also in rehearsing and refining intervention skills so that kids understand how to intervene well.

Buddy Programs in Schools and Youth Organizations

Bazelon (2013) points out that kids with high social status often make the best interveners in bullying situations because of their outsized influence on the peer group and their relative immunity from the backlash of vengeful aggressors. Their expressed disapproval of an episode of unwanted aggression sends a strong and powerful message that bullying is not cool.

Some of the most effective ally programs in schools and youth organizations are ones that build on this principle, pairing high-status kids with young people who are particularly vulnerable to bullying. These buddy programs exist all over the country and have been the subject of many touching news stories and You-Tube videos that showcase the real and enduring bonds formed between kids from opposite ends of a school social ladder. These unlikely friendships have also made clear that peer connections provide a significant measure of protection for vulnerable youth; when paired with a high-status peer, formerly bullied kids can often shed the target on their back and actually enjoy a measure of social success in their own right. For many, the experience is transformative in terms of their enjoyment of school, their ability to succeed academically, and their own self-confidence.

Jason Spector, cofounder of the antibullying organization Sweethearts and Heroes, says that most teachers in a school have at least five "soldiers" they can count on—loyal students who will always be willing to go the extra mile for that teacher (Taylor, 2013). In his presentations to educators, Spector and Sweethearts and Heroes cofounder, Tom Murphy, challenge teachers to call upon their soldiers to reach out to kids who struggle socially or are targets of bullying. They point out how effective simple acts such as sitting with vulnerable kids on the bus or walking with them in between classes can be. What's more, Spector and Murphy emphasize how important this experience is for the soldier, aka hero, as these socially astute students learn firsthand about the protective power of kindness and compassion.

An important consideration to note in developing this kind of buddy program is the totality of students who could benefit from it. While kids with moderate to severe developmental disabilities and those with pronounced physical disabilities are often invited to participate in buddy groups, kids with milder disabilities are not typically included. Social Thinking founder Michelle Garcia Winner (2013) argues that these excluded kids are often the ones who stand to gain the most from peer connections and social protection. Kids with mild disabilities often look and act just close enough to normal that no peers are actually willing to associate with them, for fear of damaging their own social status. These kids face a double abandonment then—first by their peers who think they are too quirky and then by the peer mentoring groups that don't think they are quirky enough.

Professionals who are in a position to establish a buddy program in their school or youth organization can readily find positive examples and models of such programs online. If you are considering establishing one in your school or community, think about how you can include a broad spectrum of vulnerable kids, particularly those with next-to-normal characteristics, whose lives could be significantly improved by having a genuine buddy and peer mentor.

Using Social Power Is a Process

Along with all of their academic lessons during the school-aged years, kids are learning how to use social power. Professionals and parents have a vital role to play in teaching kids just how powerful they are—that the actions they take before, during, and even after an episode of bullying can make a real difference in whether the cruelty stops short or continues mercilessly. For kids the basic message is clear: If you are present during an episode of bullying, you have the power and you own the responsibility to do something to stop it.

10 Practical Strategies to Turn Bystanders Into Allies

1. Listen to kids when they talk about their reservations related to intervening in a bullying situation.
2. Empathize with their fears and help them strategize about how to overcome obstacles to intervention.
3. Provide practical support, teaching kids assertive phrases to use to stop bullying on the spot.
4. Teach kids how to find common ground with anyone and to celebrate differences among their peers.

5. Teach kids that it is okay to stand up to a friend when that friend is behaving badly.

6. Make it known that doing nothing is not an option when they observe a bullying situation.

7. Establish a buddies program between socially mature kids and socially vulnerable ones. Monitor it. Make it rewarding for both parties.

8. Give kids a catchphrase, such as, "There is no such thing as an innocent bystander."

9. Give children the opportunity to role-play and practice bullying prevention skills. Often, these skills take finesse and need to be practiced so that they come out as intended.

10. Reinforce the message that kids have the power to make big changes in the lives of vulnerable peers and that they should never miss an opportunity to help others.

KEY 7

REACH OUT TO KIDS
WHO BULLY

I remember someone once commenting to me that aliens are the best subject for summer blockbuster movies because everyone can agree that they are the common enemy. Oftentimes, I get the impression that bullies have become the aliens of today's society: readily scorned, summarily blamed, and easily rejected. While no one is more appalled by the cruel behavior of kids who bully than me, I am guided by the words of my friend and mentor, Dr. Nicholas Long, who taught me that nothing comes from nothing and that additional scorn, blame, and rejection are the last things that wounded kids need.

Wounded kids? Bullies as victims? You might be wondering, Is this chapter going to be all about feeling sorry for kids who do reprehensible things to their peers? Not exactly. As professionals and parents poised to bring an end to bullying, the objective is not to pity kids who bully others but rather to understand why these young people behave the way they do and to use this insight to guide us in helping them change their behaviors. The paradox of bullying is that kids who push others away through their cruel behaviors and unapologetic intimidation are often kids who need others the most. When adults can see beyond surface behavior and seek to understand the pain that drives it, they have an opportunity to make a real difference in the life of a child.

What Drives Kids to Bully?

In the first key of this book, I identified elevated social status, peer attention, opportunity, and the desire for power and control as primary motivators for young people who bully their peers. In this section, we dig more deeply to understand how these motivations are really about unmet needs. Then we explore practical ways that caring adults can help make sure kids' needs are fulfilled, in turn making the kids less likely to resort to bullying.

Deficits in Emotion Management

One important consideration when looking at unmet developmental needs has to do with how young children learn to manage emotions and, specifically, express anger. Although many of us enjoy imagining the home as a sanctuary for children and families, in truth, more violence occurs domestically than in the streets (Long, Long, & Whitson, 2009). A primary source of aggression in young people, domestic violence occurs at all socioeconomic levels, across racial and ethnic lines, among both genders, and in all religions.

Kids who grow up in families in which anger and frustration are expressed through aggression often learn that expressing their own feelings in this way is the norm. Many young people feel confused, in fact, when adults in schools or treatment settings try to tell them that this method of anger expression is unacceptable; for these kids, it is all that they know.

Aggression, like bullying, is a learned behavior. That said, it can be unlearned. SEL activities that focus on teaching skills for anger management and assertive communication can make a world of difference for kids who behave like bullies outwardly, but inwardly are driven by a deficit in emotion management skills. What kids who grow up in violent, aggressive homes need is an adult who can see beyond the noise of their brutish behavior and hear their call for compassionate help.

Deficits in Decision Making and Impulse Control

One of the youths profiled in Lee Hirsch's documentary film, *Bully,* is a girl named Ja'Meya. Ja'Meya endured relentless bullying during her daily hour-long bus ride to her Mississippi school. Though she tried to reach out to adults for help, the situation worsened for her. One fateful day, Ja'Meya made a desperate decision to bring a gun from her mother's closet onto the school bus. Although she did not hurt anyone with it, she was arrested, charged with 45 felony counts, and sent to juvenile prison.

Riley, the elementary school–aged girl described in Key 1 as a victim of relational aggression, also made an impulsive decision to act out violently against the girls who were humiliating her. She, too, was seen as the sole aggressor by the authority figures who swept in to manage the situation once it had become a crisis.

Is Ja'Meya a bully? Is Riley? At a glance, both girls certainly behaved aggressively toward their peers and neither of their actions should be condoned. Both young people would benefit from learning more constructive strategies for managing impulses and making good decisions. Neither girl, however, behaved with the repetitive intent to harm others or a favorable power imbalance versus their peers that would qualify their actions as bullying. Adults play the critical role in asking the right questions and obtaining the full story before rushing to judgment and labeling any child as a bully. What you see is very infrequently what you get in most situations involving young people's social dynamics.

Deficits in Attachment

Attachment theory, originated by the work of John Bowlby, helps explain the capacity that individuals have to make enduring psychological connections. Simply put, the quality and nature of the interactions that a young child has with a primary caregiver from the earliest days of life affect the quality and nature of his relationships with others throughout the rest of his life. Kids who experience emotional deprivation and insecure attachment early on often show marked difficulties in empathy, compassion, and connectedness to others. It is not at all surprising, then, that the results of a study by the Virginia Youth Violence Project show that kids with less secure attachments to their caregivers are more likely to be identified as bullies by their peers (Eliot & Cornell, 2009).

Deficits in Belonging and Significance

Positive Parenting Solutions founder Amy McCready (2012) says that all misbehavior can be traced back to a deficit in either belonging or significance. When viewed through this lens, much of kids' bullying behavior makes sense; kids act out in ways that gain them a secure spot in their peer hierarchy. That their path to elevated social status often means demolishing someone else's group standing is part and parcel of the process; the ability to control someone else's destiny makes a child feel powerful and significant. The mystery for adults need not be why kids bully, but rather what we can do to help them achieve a sense of belonging and significance through constructive activities and behaviors rather than through bullying. Later in this key, we will talk about just that.

First, however, it is important to comprehend why some kids have such debilitating deficits in belonging and significance in the first place. The specific circumstances in which young people grow and develop without feeling adequate love or importance are as diverse as the children themselves, but these two real-life examples give a good picture of why some hurt kids hurt kids.

Anthony

By the age of 14, Anthony was 6 feet 2 inches tall, 225 pounds, and as strong as an ox. His overpowering physical presence was matched by a don't-mess-with-me attitude that intimidated everyone around him—peers and staff alike. Anthony was expelled from his regular school because of serious behavioral problems, mostly marked by aggression and fighting. In his Alternative Learning Center (ALC), Anthony was known to lie, cheat, steal, and lash out at anyone who made him angry. He was considered a bully among bullies—a thug in training, as one social worker called him—and for quite a few months, no one knew exactly how to help him.

The turning point in Anthony's treatment came one day when a teacher from the ALC saw Anthony outside of school, at a grocery store with his grandmother. His grandmother was petite and elderly—truly only half of Anthony's size. Yet her influence on the young man was supersized. The teacher reported to the ALC staff that he watched the grandmother berate Anthony verbally, in the middle of the cereal aisle at the store. Her voice was loud enough to attract the attention of shoppers across the entire store and her foul language was enough to make parents cover their kids' ears. The teacher said that several store staff came running, at first anticipating from the noise that they would need to protect a small child from a towering adult. They stopped short when they saw the opposite physical dynamic. Then, they backed away and returned to their jobs.

The last thing the teacher saw was the grandmother shoving her cart into Anthony repeatedly as she told him he was "a piece of garbage that no one else wanted" and that she was "stuck trying to feed him." Concerned about Anthony, the teacher approached the student and his grandmother, acting as if he hadn't heard their loud dispute. He identified himself as one of Anthony's teachers and asked if he could help them find anything in the aisle. Both Anthony and his grandmother declined his offer, but the distraction interrupted her aggression and the two moved on without further incident in the store.

In school on Monday, the teacher asked to speak to Anthony, as he was still concerned for his student's safety and well-being. Rather than presenting with his usual defiance, Anthony agreed to the meeting and explained in rushed sentences that he had asked his grandmother to buy him an extra box of cereal because he got so hungry at school and she was just upset because she didn't have enough money to afford all of their groceries. The teacher reported that Anthony seemed very protective of his grandmother and nervous about the conversation.

From that point forward, the staff at the ALC had an entirely new understanding of the circumstances under which Anthony was being raised. As a young man abandoned by his biological parents and left to live with an elderly, poor, abusive grandmother, Anthony was woefully lacking in core developmental experiences of being loved, wanted, and considered important. Whereas teachers at his regular school and even the ALC had been consistently focused on his aggressive behaviors and locked in constant cycles of punishment with Anthony, their new understanding of his circumstances led ALC staff members to change their focus. Now able to see Anthony's behavior as a reenactment of aggression from his home life, teachers began to approach him from a place of compassion and to try to make the ALC a safe haven in which he felt accepted and valued.

Anthony's aggressive behavior did not change overnight, nor did he get a free pass to hurt others just because the adults around him now saw his behavior in a new light. Anthony was still held accountable anytime he mistreated others, but the experience of being accepted by caring adults had a tremendous impact over the next few months and proved to be the key to changing the way this young man treated everyone around him. To see Anthony's physically imposing stature from a distance or to read about his history of repeated aggression, it would have been difficult for anyone to imagine him as a vulnerable, needy child, but that single window into his home life, serendipitously observed by a teacher in the market for some breakfast cereal, made all the difference in adults being able to understand and ultimately help change Anthony's life.

Not every child's story has such a happy ending as Anthony's, sadly. This second real-life example, however, shines light on some of the unexpected darkness in one "popular" girl's life.

Liza

Liza was the kind of girl that everyone wanted to be friends with and no one dared upset. She was pretty, athletic, popular, and seemingly in charge of the school. If you were friends with Liza, you enjoyed the trappings of her popularity, but for those who dared oppose her, she made sure they felt her wrath. Liza could single-handedly make sure that no one in the tenth grade at her school spoke, called, texted, or even looked at a girl that she did not like. She was brutal to girls' faces and merciless in her postings about them online.

Keisha was Liza's on-again, off-again best friend. From the time they were little, Keisha often played second fiddle to Liza and didn't seem to mind the role. In fact, during the times when she was unceremoniously dumped by Liza—which happened at least twice per year in middle school—Keisha would eagerly wait to get back in Liza's good graces. By high school, however, the two had drifted apart. Keisha's parents persistently encouraged her to make new friends and Liza was spending more time with boys and a faster crowd.

The news came as a shock to the whole school when Liza was found dead by her parents in her bedroom at home. Liza overdosed on a bottle of her own antidepressant medication—pills that none of her friends had a clue she was taking. Liza mailed Keisha a letter that arrived after her death. In it, she called Keisha the only true friend she had ever had. In the rest of the note, Liza lashed out at her parents for the way they "batted her back and forth" in their custody war and said that she knew that the truth was that neither of them really wanted to take care of her.

Although Liza's story ended very differently than Anthony's, what the two troubled young people shared in common was that no adult (or even child) would ever have intuited from a distance how vulnerable both of them were. Both presented themselves as strong, domineering, not-to-be-crossed figures within their peer groups, but beneath the bravado, neither one felt significant in any real way. In common, they shared an acute deficit in feeling valued by their families.

In this world, behaviors are the basis by which we judge one another. When young people behave in intentionally cruel or blatantly aggressive ways, it can be difficult for adults to feel the motivation to scratch beneath these off-putting surface behaviors. Yet the willingness to do so is the only way that kids like Anthony and Liza will be reached—and helped.

Do all kids who bully suffer from bad home lives? Certainly not. Should professionals and parents excuse bullying behavior because they become aware of a child's deprived upbringing? Not at all. Whether from nurturing, supportive families or abusive, lonely ones, the truth is that all kids have a story. When professionals and parents become willing to reach out to kids to learn what that story is all about, they offer kids choice in writing their own happier endings.

Exercise: What Developmental Needs Do You Recognize?

Think about the kids you live or work with who tend to use bullying behavior:

- Which developmental needs are fulfilled in these kids?
- Which ones are lacking?
- How does thinking about these kids in terms of unmet developmental needs change the way you feel about them?
- Will it have an impact on how you behave toward a child the next time he exhibits bullying behavior?
- How might you change your approach, yet still hold him accountable for his actions?

Mental Health Needs of Kids Who Bully

Because bullying is marked by repeated acts of aggression that intentionally harm others and is committed by individuals who hold more power than their victims, it should come as no surprise that this behavior is predictive of troubling mental health and behavioral outcomes, including substance abuse, depression, anxiety (Sourander et al., 2007), and criminal behavior (Ericson, 2001). For public health and safety reasons alone, professionals and parents should reach out to kids who bully while they are young and their behavior is still highly changeable. As the saying goes, little things become big things; when left unchecked, small acts of cruelty, minor emotional outbursts, and isolated incidents of peer manipulation can become chronic, patterned bullying behaviors that wreak havoc on homes, schools, and communities. Likewise, small acts of kindness and compassion by adults make a world of difference to kids who otherwise act out due to their feelings of being alone, devalued, and insignificant.

How to Reach Out to Kids Who Bully

Reaching out to kids who bully in order to help them change their aggressive behaviors does not have to be a complicated undertaking. Rather, as we have discussed throughout this book, some of the most impactful things that professionals and parents can do are the very simplest endeavors.

Use Positive Interventions

Many kids who engage in chronic bullying are accustomed to being cited and punished by adults for their behavior. If the first few Thou Shalt Nots did not change the young person's behavior, it stands to reason that neither will more of the same punitive actions. Even for young people who bully only on occasion, as part of a group or because of a particular social dynamic, punishment often becomes so ingrained in the routine of home or school culture that it loses its effectiveness in actually changing undesirable behavior.

Abby Potter (personal communication, May 16, 2013), of the Forbush School of Sheppard Pratt Health System in Maryland, says that to be successful in changing kids' behaviors, adults must work to create a culture of do's rather than an environment of don'ts. In a very literal sense, this might mean saying to a young child, "Please use your words to talk about how you feel," rather than scolding the child, saying, "Don't hit." On a more preventative level, adults create cultures of do's when they establish home, school, and group rules that encourage norms of respect and kindness. The hook is in setting up conditions in which kids are likely to make positive behavioral choices in the first place and then knowing specifically what changes to make if they do make a mistake.

Exercise: Creating a Culture of Do's

Think about the types of bullying situations that are most typical in your life or work with kids. Write down at least three recent events that caused you concern. For each one, consider a positive intervention you could use to reach out to the child who bullied and encourage her to make different choices in the way they she interacts with her peers.

How would this positive intervention compare with a punitive one? With the particular child in mind, think about how her responses might differ, based on your use of either a "do" or a "don't."

Begin from a Place of Kindness

Longtime educator and Life Space Crisis Intervention Institute founder Dr. Nicholas Long says that if self-absorbed young people are to contribute to the world, they must first experience kindness—even when their behavior suggests they may not deserve it. In fact, Long calls kindness "the most powerful tool that adults have in their arsenal for transforming youth with problems into youth with promise" (Brokenleg & Long, 2013).

Kindness does not necessarily always come naturally to professionals or parents after they have witnessed or become aware of a young person committing a cruel act. Yet it is only by beginning from a place of kindness that a child will feel valued and supported enough to become willing to examine his behavior or begin to make changes in it. When young people are approached by adults who are ready to listen, they tend to talk. When they are approached by adults who are ready to accuse, they tend to become defensive and deny wrongdoing. The decision is really up to the adult: How do you want your conversation with a child to go?

Exercise: The Authority Figures in Your Life

Part of growing up means going head-to-head with authority figures. For kids, getting along with some adults comes as naturally as breathing, but with other grown-ups, clashes seem unavoidable. Think about the authority figures in your life when you were a child. Consider the following:

- What type of adult was always easy for you to talk to, confide in, and even admit your wrongdoings?
- What specific behaviors did that adult use to make you feel safe, supported, and valued?
- How would you describe the authority figures that made you defensive, angry, or frustrated?
- Which of their behaviors turned you off or turned you away?
- How do you want to be remembered by a young person, when he thinks back on the authority figures from his childhood?

Listen Well

As noted in Key 1, only a small fraction of bullying takes place in front of adults. Therefore, most of the information an adult receives about unwanted aggression arrives secondhand. It is not uncommon for authority figures to begin a conversation with a child who is accused of bullying with a very strong—if not completely convinced—preconceived notion of the child's guilt. Under these conditions, it is very challenging for an adult to listen well. Rather, many adults listen exclusively for the facts that confirm their preset agenda.

Unfortunately, this sets the stage for further alienation in the accused bully. When the child senses that the adult is not really interested in his story or making a genuine attempt to gather his point of view, he often shuts down. Important details about the child's perceptions and thoughts are missed, as is a real opportunity to connect.

Returning to the lives of Ja'Meya and Riley, it is clear that there is rarely such a thing as a clear-cut case of bullying and that sometimes the obvious aggressor is actually a hidden victim. What may look like a slam-dunk case for the prosecution often involves layers and layers of detail that are important to understanding the whole crime scene. Yes, sometimes, all of those layers point conclusively to a child acting like a bully, pure and simple. But other times, there is a vital backstory. The only way adults will ever have a chance of learning that story is if they commit to listening well in every instance.

Replace the Rush

In Key 6, we talked about the dopamine rush that some young people experience when they bully. The heightened sense of power and boost in social status that kids derive from bullying can be highly reinforcing. Adults can make a positive impact on bringing an end to bullying when they help kids find alternate ways to experience the boost to their brain's reward centers. Does playing a sport enhance a child's popularity in a healthier way than bullying a vulnerable child does? Will performing in a play give a young girl the positive attention she craves? Does a child feel good when participating in martial arts? Dance? Volunteering? An after-school job? For each child, the answer will be different, but anything that provides a young person with positive feedback is reinforcing. Connected adults can help kids discern the particular activities that will channel their strengths and point them down a positive path.

Fulfill Unmet Needs

This is not meant to serve as a catch-all category but rather as an important reminder that all behavior is purposeful. Kids act—and act out—in order to fulfill certain needs. Adults play a key role in making sure that vital developmental needs of young people are consistently met.

Belonging

For a child who has deficits in belonging, adults can focus efforts on making the young person feel included, accepted, and welcomed into various groups. Whether it is at home among family members or at school in the cafeteria, in class, on a team, or within a club, kids benefit tremendously from everyday experiences of feeling that they fit in and belong. Something as seemingly insignificant as spending 10 minutes of uninterrupted time with a child each day or making sure to greet her by name each morning when she walks into school are practical and highly meaningful ways that adults can give kids a sense of belonging.

Personal Power

If a young person bullies as a way of experiencing personal power, parents can reach out by providing her with meaningful ways to contribute to the family and professionals can structure opportunities at school for the child to have some autonomy, show leadership among peers, and make independent decisions. The buddy programs described in Key 6 are a perfect example of how to help foster positive power in a socially astute child by giving her the responsibility to mentor and protect a socially vulnerable one.

Empathy

Many kids who bully have deficits in empathy. As discussed in Key 5, focused SEL programming can go a long way in helping young people develop increased empathy toward their peers. A far more powerful way for a child to learn empathy for others, however, is by experiencing genuine empathy from others. Consider your own life experience: How did you learn to be empathic? Did you learn this quality from reading about it in a book? Did you memorize it like you would a math fact? Chances are excellent that neither of the above occurred, but rather you learned empathy because a few key adults in your life responded empathically to you during your times of need. Indeed, adults who consistently approach kids from a place of kindness and compassion role model and teach empathy in the most genuine ways.

Exercise: Coping With Conflict and Managing Anger

Kids who bully often have weak conflict resolution and emotion management skills. Think of a child with whom you live or work that struggles to resolve conflicts with peers or manage emotions. Write down at least three practical ways that you can help meet these unfilled needs for this child.

What Does Not Work When Reaching Out to Kids Who Bully

Bazelon (2013) notes that one of the biggest dangers of bullying prevention activities is the "zeal to punish." Call it a media-induced race for a sound bite or a busy person's need to cross an item off of a to-do list; singling out a sole aggressor and holding him or her up as an example of what happens to kids who behave badly usually has a lot more to do with fulfilling an adult's need to win than with meeting a child's need to learn, make amends, and grow. An important caution for adults involved in the discipline side of bullying prevention is to make sure their activities are aimed at long-term behavioral change for the child rather than short-term satisfaction for onlookers.

In this final section of the chapter, we look at four categories of discipline that tend to be ineffective in reaching and changing the behaviors of kids who bully.

Zero Tolerance and Expulsion

Zero tolerance is the most widely used discipline policy in U.S. schools. It is based on assigning predetermined punishments for infractions of school rules, without regard to circumstances or context. In its purest form, it is expedient, grounded in equality, and based on the philosophy that justice is blind.

In its practical application, however, zero tolerance often has the unintended consequence of making matters worse. When it comes to bullying, studies show that removing kids who bully from schools does not help them, but rather predicts higher rates of future misbehavior and suspension (Espelage & Swearer, 2010). If effectively helping kids is grounded in establishing meaningful connections, then severing those connections through zero tolerance and expulsion ensures greater feelings of alienation, insignificance, and all of the developmental deficits that fuel bullying in the first place. When it comes to zero tolerance, the punishment is implicated in the cause of the crime.

Peer Mediation

I am all for peer mediation programs. Just not for kids who bully. I think peer mediation programs teach many kids valuable skills for conflict resolution and respectful problem solving. But for kids who bully, peer mediation can become a virtual stage for sanctioned peer domination. In front of trained peer mediators, school counselors, teachers, and any other welcomed spectators, socially astute kids who bully get to enjoy the predictable rush of dopamine as they outtalk and outwit their less savvy target. If the bullied child cries when he comes face to face with his bully, it is all the more reinforcing for the child with deficits in empathy; he does not feel remorse in the moment, but rather feels empowered by the deep way he has affected his peer. In this scenario, consider how one peer mediation event impacts two middle school boys in very different ways:

Justin's middle school had a peer mediation program that was popular among the administrative staff but ridiculed by most of the student body. Save for the small handful of eighth grade students who were hand selected by the principal to be peer mediators, the other students regarded the program as a joke. To be sent to peer mediation was as good as being publicly branded a baby and to follow the recommendations of the peer mediators was about as uncool as a kid could get.

So when Justin reluctantly admitted to his parents that the rip in his new winter coat was the result of a fight on the bus with Logan, and his parents reported the incident to the principal, the kids in his homeroom laughed out loud when he and Logan were both called via the PA system to report to the office. "Peer mediation!" they all mocked knowingly.

As a standard part of a peer mediation, both parties must agree to take part in the event. In front of the school counselor and two eighth grade mediators, Logan agreed readily. Justin, on the other hand, said he did not want to participate in a mediation. When asked why not, he didn't answer. When asked again in private by the school counselor, Justin explained that Logan picked on him every single day on the bus and that he knew mediation was not going to change anything. "It's just going to make it worse for me," he argued. The school counselor argued back, "If you are saying you are not willing to participate in this process, then you're saying you don't want things to get better. He's trying to do the right thing, Justin. As far as I have observed, you are the one who is not cooperating here. Is this what you want me to report back to your parents?"

Feeling coerced, Justin returned with the school counselor to the mediation room. He told his side of the story when asked. Logan listened without speaking. When Logan was given his chance to speak, he admitted all of the things he did, but explained that his actions were simply attempts to try to get Justin to open up more on the bus. "You know, I'm trying to get him to laugh and goof around with the rest of us. I just want to help him make some friends. You know, he is considered a total loser on the bus," Logan continued, "and I was trying to involve him in more of our conversation so he could fit in. I guess it's just not going to happen for him. He'd rather have everyone continue to see him as a big-time dork."

At that point, one of the eighth grade mediators stepped in with a quick reminder not to use the word "dork," but then allowed Logan to continue with his passive-aggressive defamation of Justin, under the guise of "trying to help" his target. At the end of it all, the two boys were asked to apologize to one another and shake hands. No consequences were administered to either boy, no admonishments were given for past behavior, and no advice was provided for their future interactions in school or on the bus.

Justin felt even more humiliated than ever. He had been called out in front of his homeroom peers to attend a peer mediation, pressured to participate in the event by the school counselor, made to sit through Logan's public shaming, and had gained absolutely nothing from any of it. As they walked out of the room, Logan followed Justin, stepping on his heels as they walked out of the school office, and whispered, "See you on the bus, sucker."

This instance with Justin and Logan is all too typical of peer mediation events conducted between kids who bully and their carefully selected targets. Peer mediators may feel good after a mediation event, believing that they have shown leadership at a school event. Adults may feel good, relieved that they can check an item off their agenda. Kids who bully likely feel great, self-satisfied at having won. The child who was bullied—the one that the mediation was intended to help—feels more demoralized than ever, for now he knows for certain that there is no one in the school who can see through the bully's socially astute facade and nobody that will protect him from future abuse at the hands of his slick-talking aggressor.

Social Skills Groups Populated Solely by Kids Who Bully

As detailed in Key 5, kids who bully can benefit tremendously from SEL programming focused on empathy development, emotion management, social skills, and so on. The composition of these small groups, however, must be carefully structured by adults. When kids who bully are homogeneously gathered together with the good intention of being taught prosocial skills, what they more often do is learn from each other new strategies to dominate others. No empathy skills are gained when each member's sole purpose is to push the other ones down a peg. When all of the alpha players are together in a room, peer-control efforts run amuck.

Restorative Justice

Restorative justice is an approach increasingly being sought by schools looking for alternatives to zero tolerance and expulsion. Its goal is to encourage young people to develop empathy for one another by engaging in face-to-face dialogue in which they come up with plans for accountability and reparation. For adults and kids alike, restorative justice has been shown to be transformative (Centre for Justice and Reconciliation, 2008).

In the dynamics of bullying, however, where major power im-balances are at work, this approach is less effective, according to Barbara McClung, behavioral health manager of the Oakland Unified School District (Brown, 2013). As with peer mediation, restorative justice cannot work properly if a socially powerful child is unwilling to acknowledge or sincerely attempt to repair the harm he or she has caused.

A Challenge for Readers

Many great organizations and individuals are actively working to bring an end to bullying by providing insightful strategies for kids on how to cope with bullying and teaching bystanders to stand up for victims everywhere. Many experts teach that stopping bullying begins with empowering bystanders (I agree) and explain that changing the behavior of a child who bullies is the most difficult course of action (I agree again).

Where I differ with these experts, however—and I hope to in-spire you to do the same—is in the philosophy that because a child's bullying behavior is difficult to change that we should abandon our efforts to do so. In my years of working with troubled kids as a social worker and therapist, I have learned two facts that have taught me otherwise:

1. The young people who are the best at alienating adults are truly the children who need adult connections the most.
2. As a helper, you may not be able to reach all of the kids with whom you meet, but you never know whose life you could help transform, so you have to try with every single one.

As you ponder your role in bringing an end to bullying, I chal-lenge you to think about the profoundly positive impact you could have on all kids—especially the ones you never expected to be able to help.

10 Practical Strategies to Reach Out to Kids Who Bully

1. Be willing to look beyond behavior to understand the thoughts, feelings, experiences, and perceptions that drive each child's actions.

2. Teach kids skills for healthy emotion management and assertive communication.

3. Practice constructive problem solving with kids who bully. Focus on positive, win-win ways to deal with peer conflict.

4. Intervene early in the lives of children who bully to help change negative behavior patterns and prevent chronic mental health problems.

5. Do everything you can to give a young person a strong sense of belonging.

6. Greet all children by name and with a smile every time they walk into your home, classroom, or group to help them feel connected and valued.

7. Structure opportunities for young people to exercise compassionate peer leadership in ways that benefit all kids.

8. "Glance at problems; gaze at strengths" (Chambers, 2012). Hold kids accountable for negative behaviors, but spend most of your time cultivating their positive personal traits and prosocial behaviors.

9. Create a culture of do's rather than an environment of don'ts.

10. Approach kids from a place of kindness always—even when their behaviors might not inspire it.

KEEP THE CONVERSATION GOING

Not long ago, a friend and former colleague confided in me that she was all set to begin using my *Friendship and Other Weapons* (Whitson, 2011a) curriculum in her parochial elementary school when word came down from school administrators that "the school doesn't want to talk to the kids about bullying. It implies that there is a problem."

Open sandbox, insert head.

Some adults, like the ones at this school, choose to turn a blind eye to the problem of bullying because they want to save face in their communities, even at the expense of doing right by the children they are trusted to serve. Others deny bullying for very opposite reasons: They care so deeply about the well-being of young people that finding out that their interventions have not been effective is simply too painful to hear.

In the documentary film *Bully*, Alex is a young man who reaches out to school staff for help in handling relentless tormenting by a peer. In one particular instance, Alex reported that a peer sat on his head, but told filmmakers in frustration that "nothing was done about it." When questioned about Alex's report, the school administrator had a very different view of her managing of the incident, insisting that she did intervene by talking to the aggressor and that, indeed, she had fixed the problem. In her eyes, the fact that the child did not sit on Alex's head again was proof positive of the progress that she had made. That the aggressive child continued to bully Alex in countless other ways seemed irrelevant to her. Aside from her quick, isolated talk with the child who bullied, there was no follow-up to confirm her intervention's effectiveness. Rather, the adult was operating on what I call the "intervene and hope" model. As child development specialist Dr. Robyn Silverman (2012) points out, "ignorance may be bliss, but it's not effective in counteracting bullying."

Perhaps this school administrator's problem was one of feeling helpless. With movie cameras rolling, her professional reputation on the line, and a child's well-being at stake, she felt compelled to find a quick fix and pressured to have it be effective. It could well be that following up on the proposed solution—only to find that the problem had changed shape (read: grown bigger)—would have created unmanageable feelings of helplessness for her, so she figured that it was better not to follow up at all.

Sadly, this adult is not alone in responding this way. Many adults who desperately and genuinely want to do right by kids give up on even attempting to manage incidents of bullying because they feel so overwhelmed by the complexity of the challenge and so professionally humbled by the task. Convincing themselves that the problem either doesn't exist or is readily solved by a single intervention brings their anxiety level back down. Whether or not a vulnerable young person is actually made safer falls by the wayside.

There are also adults who operate strictly from a risk management perspective. These adults don't worry much about improving the school culture for kids but do care an awful lot about their own livelihoods. For them, going through the motions of intervening in a bullying situation is enough, even if their intervention is ineffective, insincere, or insufficient. From a legal standpoint, these adults can honestly say that they fulfilled the precise obligations dictated by their school or organization's antibullying policy and so their conscience is clear. In other words, they don't want to talk about it anymore.

Adults have to get beyond local politics, school policies, and personal insecurities in order to truly be there for young people.

When there is denial of the problem, kids cannot be safe. They cannot learn and they cannot develop skills for managing the conflict that is an inevitable part of being human. On the other hand, opening up a dialogue about conflict, about friendships, and about how to successfully navigate the sometimes-choppy waters of both is a simple way to show kids that you understand what is important in their world and that you care enough to listen to their experiences. In the final key of this book, we talk about strategies for maintaining an open dialogue on bullying and insisting on focused, effective interventions that will help bring a real end to this problem.

Are We Just Talking About It More?

In both my scheduled workshops and my casual conversations on the topic of bullying, professionals and parents often ask me, "Is bullying really worse today than it was when we were kids, or are we just talking about it more?"

My answer to that question is an emphatic "Yes."

The round-the-clock availability of cell phones, texting, e-mails, and social networking sites have intensified the impact of bullying, giving young people private ways to humiliate each other and public ways to spread rumors to large-scale audiences. At the same time, groundbreaking books, films, and media coverage have shone a spotlight on a phenomenon that existed too often in secret for generations.

When I first waded into the waters of bullying, my instincts told me that I was exploring uncharted territory—that the bullying that was occurring in this day and age was qualitatively different, and worse, than anything any other generation had ever experienced. While it's fun to feel like a pioneer, I humbly see things differently now. Countless adults have generously shared with me their experiences of having been bullied in their elementary, middle, and high school years—sometimes as long as 40 years ago—and while you might expect that their pain would be tempered after years of life experience and the benefit of adult perspective, over and over again their retelling of tales of cruelty brings up emotion that is as raw as what I hear from the current generation of young people. I am now convinced that bullying has been unbearable for its victims for as long as kids have been cruel and that talking about it, whether in the moment or decades later, is important. Recent research, publications, and media attention to bullying have given untold numbers of victims—past and present—a voice to share their experiences, now that they finally realize that they are not alone.

"Are we just talking about it more?" people ask me.

"Yes," I answer. "Finally, we are talking about it more!"

Now, there is often a difference between the question being spoken and the question being asked. I understand that when some professionals or parents ask me "Are we just talking about it more?" their question is coming from a place of skepticism; what they really want to know is, "Are we just making a big deal out of nothing?"

Interestingly, I rarely get the opportunity to have first dibs on answering this roundabout question. Whenever it is asked in a group setting, parents who have walked through the fires of bullying alongside their child are first to stand up and give their emotional, heart-wrenching testimonials about how relentless and viral today's bullying can be. I challenge anyone to maintain a "kids will be kids" mentality after hearing a mother describe how her daughter receives nightly text messages saying, "kill yourself and get it over with already." I have yet to witness any workshop attendee maintain his skepticism about how deeply bullying can wound after listening to a 14-year-old girl confess to her failed suicide attempt—her desperate response to three endless years of being called a "whore" (she is a virgin) and a "druggie" (she has never used drugs) by her "friends" at school.

Rather than becoming accustomed to the stories I hear from kids, parents, teachers, and counselors, I am instead more troubled and appalled every day by the types of aggression that young people face. "Are we just making a big deal out of nothing?" some people may imply. "Not on your life," eyewitnesses confirm. Maintaining an open dialogue about bullying and making sure that we continue to shine a bright light on this once-shadowed topic is the only way that we will be able to hold adults and kids accountable for bringing an end to this long-standing problem.

What Parents Can Do When Bullying Is Downplayed at School

Another common theme I hear from parents on the topic of bullying is their frustration—too often their desperation—at reporting incidents of genuine bullying to school staff and having those reports downplayed or outright dismissed. Despite the "Bully-Free Zone" posters that line their school's cafeteria walls and the zero-tolerance policy that was boasted about during the autumn back-to-school night, many parents report that their actual experience is that their child's school would rather not address the problem at all. They say that the responses they get from their kid's teachers or school administrators include bland lip service such as:

- I didn't see it happening and I can't just take your child's word that it did.
- Kids will be kids, you know.
- This stuff just happens. It'll all blow over soon.
- Your child just needs to have a thicker skin.
- The child you are accusing of bullying is an honor student and vice president of the student council. I just can't believe she would do such a thing. Are you sure your child isn't exaggerating?

Here's the thing: by the time a young person has mustered the courage to tell an adult about the torment she has suffered at the hands of a peer, she has usually already exhausted all of her coping skills. The child has practiced ignoring the bully, avoiding her tormentors, standing up to mean kids in assertive ways, enlisting a friend's support, and using humor to deflect the bully's taunting. The young person has shut down her Facebook page and stopped texting entirely, hoping that taking herself out of the technology loop might give her some respite from the cruelty. Yet the bullying persists. The child is now feeling powerless, distressed, and perhaps even a bit distrustful of all of the advice she has received from adults about how to cope with bullying on her own, since none of it has worked. Still, she decides to take the chance—to risk the humiliation and feelings of shame—and to reach out to tell her parents about how everyone at school has turned against her.

The parent makes a decision to call the child's teacher and report what has been going on—the name calling, the cruel texts, the exclusion at lunch, the snickering in the halls, the shoves on the bus, and the threats of physical harm (yesterday's warning: "I am going to f'ing end you if you come to school tomorrow"). Reaching out and asking for help is hard for many parents. Protective caregivers have a deep need to believe that they can single-handedly make things right for their kids. Confident, however, that they have taken all of the right steps to manage their child's problem independently and knowing that the bullying (and their child's desperation) are only getting worse, the parents reluctantly place a call to the school. Many of these parents have told me that a part of them was initially relieved when they finally decided to share their child's burden with professionals.

Too often, their relief is short-lived.

More and more, as I talk with parents whose children have experienced bullying, they share this common experience of having their concerns downplayed by the very adults who are charged with keeping schoolchildren safe. Parents ask me: What should I do when I report bullying to the school and the school downplays my concerns?

This is the conversation we usually have. First, we talk a bit about why some school personnel downplay reports of bullying from concerned parents. We talk about all of the obstacles to bringing an end to bullying that I described in Key 1, including how easy it can be for school staff to miss incidents of well-hidden aggression, how never-ending to-do lists can diminish a teacher's availability to intervene, how the "kids will be kids" mentality allows some adults to minimize the problem of bullying, and how feelings of helplessness often overwhelm otherwise caring and well-intentioned adults.

After talking about the various reasons why some adults downplay reports of bullying, I like to work with parents to strategize about realistic approaches for pursuing the attention and focus of school personnel. The point I make most strongly is that it takes a tremendous amount of courage for most kids to talk with their parents about being the target of bullying. It is such a deeply painful and humiliating experience that even kids with the most trusting relationship with their parents find their victimization hard to reveal. Therefore, when kids do talk about being bullied, it is imperative that parents honor the courageous act of sharing and become their child's champion.

I'm not exaggerating when I tell parents to don their hero's cape and get ready to be superhuman, because in many cases, that is what challenging the status quo will take. In every case, that is what their child deserves. So, what can parents do when their report of bullying is downplayed by school personnel?

Talk, Talk, Talk

A bully's preferred method of intimidation is to keep the victim isolated. A parent's best strategy for countering bullying is to reach out to as many people as necessary to make sure that the bullying comes to an end. If you have reached out to your child's teacher and received a bland, disinterested, or downplayed response, do not be deterred. Continue to contact other school personnel—preferably according to a chain of command—to make sure that your voice (and more importantly, your child's voice) is heard.

Rather than making emotional demands for an on-the-spot meeting with a school official, parents and caregivers should maintain a level head and call to schedule an appointment with the teacher, guidance counselor, school social worker, principal—or all of the above. If their concerns or their child's needs continue to be unmet, parents should then turn to the school's parent-teacher organization, the local school board, the district superintendent, or even the local police if the parents are concerned about their child's safety.

Parents should also talk to their neighbors and fellow parents about what is going on. I remind parents not to bash the school or gossip about the children who are doing the bullying in a way that tarnishes their own integrity, but rather to make sure to enlist the help of everyone and anyone that is in a position to address the situation and help bring the bullying to an end.

Another course of action I recommend to some parents is to take their concerns online. The blogging community can be a rich source of support, guidance, and been-there-done-that practical advice for parents whose kids are being bullied. Likewise, the media has taken a growing interest in the problem of bullying. If parents can't convince school personnel to take a stand, perhaps the media can. Bullying prevention author Jacqui DiMarco (2011) advises parents to "be the most pleasant nuisance you possibly can be until you have resolution."

Document, Document, Document

It is critical that parents and caregivers write down their child's account of the incidents of bullying. They should record as much detail as possible, since memory tends to be short and details can easily and understandably be distorted by emotion. When parents contact the staff at their child's school, they should make notes on whom they talk to and when. Parents who are serious about bringing about change for their child should document the school personnel's responses—word for word, whenever possible. Prior to meeting with a teacher, counselor, or principal, parents should also write down their goals for the conversation. Afterward, they are wise to put in writing any agreed-upon resolutions and request that all involved parties sign the document to indicate their agreement.

Documenting conversations, decisions, and agreed-upon plans of action help keep parents and school personnel on the same page during what can be an emotional time. Establishing a paper trail is not a "gotcha!" process, but rather an effective way of keeping all involved parties organized, informed, and goal directed.

For parents of children who have an Individualized Education Program (IEP), consider requesting that a goal about bullying be included in your child's plan. Be clear in phrasing the goal, including specific actions that school staff will take when they become informed about bullying activities. IEPs are legal documents and, as such, they are taken very seriously by schools. Establishing a legal plan of action related to bullying is an important level of protection for parents and kids. What's more, inclusion in an IEP will ensure that the topic of bullying—and your goal of bringing it to an end—will be revisited each time an IEP meeting occurs for your child.

Persist, Persist, Persist

Simmons (2011) writes that when a child doesn't think her situation will improve, the strength that her parents show can be hugely reassuring. Indeed, a show of resolve and dogged determination to persist until their concerns are adequately addressed is among the most important things parents can do for their children. This willingness to keep at it communicates to kids that their concerns are valid, their safety is paramount, and that they are worthy of your time and effort.

Remember, by the time a child has told a parent about the bullying she is facing, she has in all likelihood been dealing with the problem for quite some time and is feeling worn down and demoralized. When a parent shows that she believes what her child has reported, takes the concerns seriously, and is willing to persistently stand up for her child, the child's self-worth can begin to grow again.

Public service announcements and posters that tell victims to speak up in the face of bullying mean nothing at all if, when kids and families find the courage to speak up, they are met with disbelief, denial, and downplaying by school staff. What kind of message are adults sending? What better way is there to violate a child's trust and create a sense of hopelessness and helplessness? Adults cannot continue to fail children in this way.

A controversial step chosen by some parents is to ask school administrators to allow their children to switch out of particular classes in which they are being bullied or to switch schools altogether if they are being relentlessly targeted by multiple peers. Those who are against removing students from troublesome situations argue that kids need to learn to deal directly with bullying. A parent I interviewed insisted, "In real life, you can't always escape a bad situation with a neighbor or at work, so kids need to learn that they can't run away from their troubles." While it is certainly true that kids benefit from developing skills to manage conflict independently, it is equally true that there is no gain in keeping young people in powerless positions.

Indeed, changing schools or removing young people from certain classes is not about bubble-wrapping them from all adversity; it is about a trustworthy and compassionate adult standing up and taking definitive action to keep a young person physically, emotionally, and psychologically safe. While I would not recommend that parents take this step lightly or make switching schools a first response to peer conflict, I do support taking decisive action as necessary to remove kids from damaging peer dynamics. In the case of this high school sophomore, it was an action that saved his life:

> Tucker was a 15-year-old student attending a conservative Christian high school. The teachers and staff of the school believed adamantly that homosexuality was a sin, so while they were quite good at teaching compassion and tolerance as part of their general school values, they actively looked the other way when kids used derogatory language about gay people.
>
> For as long as he could recall, Tucker remembered kids

telling him that he was going to grow up to be a homosexual because he took part in various community theater activities. By the time he got to high school, bullying about his sexual identity had become vicious—from physical assaults in the locker room in which kids accused him of staring at them in the shower to almost constant verbal taunting and threats of violence. Tucker dreaded school every day. His grades dropped, he lost weight, and he had difficulty sleeping at night.

In elementary and middle school, Tucker tried to cope with the bullying on his own, but by his freshman year in high school, he was overwhelmed and decided to confide in his parents about what had been going on. At first, they down-played his reports and instructed him to ignore the other kids. When they saw his grades drop and his increasing alienation from friends, however, they took all of the right steps to contact school personnel, ask for action by teachers, and demand safety for their son. Tucker's parents had both graduated from the same Christian high school themselves and were active member of its PTO. They were quick to defend the school staff and slow to reach the conclusion that the school was not a healthy environment for their son, but after 18 months of bland lip service to their many specific, documented reports of physical, verbal, and cyberbullying, Tucker's parents came to the heart-wrenching decision to remove their son from the school.

Tucker transferred in the middle of his tenth grade year to a public school in a neighboring town. In his own words, he "never looked back." His grades returned to honor roll, his weight returned to normal, he rediscovered the adolescent joys of sleeping in, and he found a supportive group of friends. Tucker said that he still was the target of gay slurs from time to time, even at the new school, but he felt safe knowing that the new school staff would intervene when they found out about it and that most of his friends had his back whenever he was targeted.

At a celebratory lunch, following his high school graduation ceremony, Tucker told his parents that the best thing they
ever did for him was transfer him out of the Christian high
school. When asked why this was such an important change,
he said that he knew the move was really difficult for his
parents because of their deep connections to the school, but
that their willingness to go the extra mile to keep him safe was
the most supported he had ever felt in his whole life.

He also revealed to his parents for the first time that during
his sophomore year, he had seriously contemplated suicide as
a means to escape the bullying he had endured for so many
years. He explained, "Before I knew that changing schools was
an option, I didn't think I had any way out of the daily torture.
The only thing I did know was that I couldn't live like that
anymore. Leaving that school showed me that there was a
whole different happiness and sense of peace that I could
experience. It made me feel like I actually wanted to live
again. I had totally lost that desire up till that point."

Exercise: What Can You Do to Be a Champion for a Child?

Have you been in a situation where you needed to advocate for
a child's rights or needs? What was the situation? How did you go
about ensuring that proper action was taken on behalf of the child,
no matter what the obstacles? How can you apply these lessons to
helping a child get the help he needs in managing a bullying situation?

What Schools Can Do to Keep
the Conversation About Bullying Going

Schools and other youth-serving organizations play a vital role in
keeping the issue of bullying on the forefront of people's minds. If
they are wise, they will do it in a way that focuses conversations on

ongoing prevention efforts and the steady cultivation of respectful group cultures, rather than on the more media-friendly reactive, punitive, crisis-oriented stories. As I bring this book to a close, I focus on three practical strategies that schools and youth-serving organizations can employ to make bringing an end to bullying a consistent topic of conversation, and one that is intentionally focused on positive solutions.

Conduct School-Wide Surveys

As the saying goes, what gets assessed gets addressed. One of the best ways for schools to gather, analyze, and knowledgeably act on information about school climate, peer relationships, and bullying activity is to conduct regular surveys of both students and staff. The Harvard Graduate School of Education (2013) recommends these strategies for using surveys effectively:

- Schools should conduct surveys two or three times per year. Surveys should be administered early in the school year and then again at the midpoint or at the end of the year to assess progress and adjust interventions based on results.
- Survey questions should address:
  * How often, when, and where bullying occurs
  * Whether students have peers and adults they trust
  * Whether students and staff believe the school lives up to its stated values
  * Whether students have symptoms of depression, anxiety, or loneliness
- Surveys can be short, and conducted anonymously with students and staff.
- Schools should designate a leadership group of administrators, staff, parents, and students (when possible) to review the data and make an action plan.
- Results should be shared with the entire school community to create impetus for change and to establish genuine accountability.

Any school stands to benefit from the use of a school-wide bullying survey—not just those who are already aware that they have a problem with bullying. One of the greatest gains of using a survey, in fact, is when school staff who were previously unaware of existing bullying dynamics learn about what is really brewing under the surface of their status quo.

For those who might worry about stirring the pot, be assured that comprehensive, anonymous surveys do not cause bullying, nor do they create false positives. Rather, good information-gathering methods can pull back the curtain on well-hidden aggression that, if left unexposed, would erode the culture of the entire student body.

Plan Events for Students, Faculty, Parents, and Community Members

School-wide events pull people together. From the planners to the participators and everyone in between, when schools dedicate time and resources to hosting an event, they make a strong statement about where they place their values. What could be more important for a school than to declare with pride that it prioritizes the physical, emotional, and social well-being of its students? School-wide events can be large scale or small group, festive or serious, costly or free. Ideas for school-sponsored bullying prevention activities that keep students, faculty, parents, and community members all talking about bullying include the following.

In-Service Training for Staff

Professional staff have to attend a required number of continuing education days each school year. While most of these days are focused on strictly academic matters, there is still ample time for equipping educators with skills that empower them to understand, recognize, and respond effectively to bullying in schools. Ideally, these in-service opportunities should go beyond rote policy reviews and truly engage teachers with practical strategies, easy-to-implement classroom strategies, and the confidence that their daily actions can and will make a difference in changing the culture of bullying in their schools.

A school may choose to have antibullying training led by a professional expert from outside the school. Sometimes outsiders are best equipped to energize, inspire, offer fresh perspectives, and teach new ideas to staff. On the other hand, people coming in from outside a school or organization do not always have the benefit of audience members' trust. Staff often are skeptical that a hired consultant will know enough about their particular group to be able to make relevant recommendations. And let's be honest: some professionals are just plain sick and tired of "experts" coming in from the outside to tell them how to do their jobs.

Very often, a member of the school community who is well educated about bullying and bullying prevention is in an ideal position to lead in-service training for staff on how to intervene effectively in the school. Another clear benefit of this inside facilitator is that he or she can provide guidance and consultation to colleagues at any given point during the school year. Last, of course, in-house trainers tend to be highly cost-effective for budget-strapped schools.

Educators may also choose to partner with other schools and professionals in their area for bullying prevention training. Strategic partnerships are a great way to pool resources and benefit from the sharing of new ideas. Small conferences that feature several different presenters can be a great way to offer multiple perspectives on bullying and varied intervention ideas while at the same time serving as a great public relations opportunity for schools to demonstrate to their entire community their commitment to bringing an end to bullying.

Assemblies for Kids
There are all kinds of possibilities when it comes to planning school-wide assemblies for students. Young kids often love author visits when writers read aloud their fictional stories about bullying,

engage kids in exciting learning activities, and autograph their books as a memorable keepsake. Upper elementary and middle school students are sometimes a tough crowd for traditional talk presentations but can be meaningfully engaged by experiential presenters who involve them in the assembly and challenge them to think about bullying in brand new ways. For example, presentations that focus on practical ways that bystanders can become allies give kids much-needed skills and can be particularly empowering to audiences craving realistic ways to act when they see bullying happening. High school kids may benefit most from presentations that focus on the impact of technology on peer relationships and that provide realistic information about legal issues related to cyberbullying.

A list of presenters and organizations that offer in-service training for educators and assemblies for kids is provided in the Resources section of this book.

Community Forums for Parents

Opportunities for parents and caregivers to become well informed about bullying are often less abundant than those provided for professionals and kids. A school's PTO is the perfect group to sponsor community educational forums that focus on providing information and, perhaps as importantly, building a sense of partnership between school staff and parents. While typical dynamics pit parents and educators against each other when it comes to addressing incidents of bullying in schools, the use of educational forums can bring all adults together, by establishing an ongoing dialogue, a common language, and a set of shared goals. When parents and schools function as partners, kids win.

Moreover, parents often function in isolation from each other. While kids interact daily in school, their parents seldom meet and rarely interact. School-sponsored educational forums give parents the chance to meet, talk, align themselves in a common cause to end bullying, and feel like they are not all alone in their efforts to support their kids.

Special Screenings

When the 2012 documentary *Bully* was released, so too was launched the Bully Project's 1 Million Kids campaign, an effort to share the film with at least one million students. Schools everywhere were invited to schedule screenings of the film with students and staff and were provided with free materials to guide large-group discussions. Professionals continue to be encouraged to screen the documentary with groups of middle and high school–aged kids and use it as a springboard for important conversations about bullying. The real-life stories in the film provide compelling fodder for group discussion and self-reflection. While much of the content in the film is painful to watch, this emotionality is exactly what makes *Bully* impactful for kids and ideally suited for discussion groups. Information on planning a film showing and discussion is available at www.thebullyproject .com.

Empower Student-Led Initiatives

Often the best source of ideas about what will or won't work when it comes to stopping bullying is kids themselves. After all, young people are the true experts when it comes to knowing the ins and outs of the social dynamics of their school. Likewise, students are in the best position to understand the types of initiatives that will genuinely speak to their peers and inspire them to sincerely change bullying behaviors.

Researchers have found that in order for student-led initiatives to be effective, two conditions should be met (Collier, Swearer, Doces, & Jones, 2012):

1. Student-led initiatives work best when students are engaged with and supported by a competent, trained adult.
2. Students who can engage with and motivate a diverse group of other students tend to be more effective than those who try to operate on their own.

Another consideration for adults is to try to space the rolling out of student-led initiatives throughout the school year, rather than bunching them all up at a single time of the year. Antibullying initiatives function best as consistent messages, wrapped into the daily life of students, rather than as a brief flurry of activity focused around a single bullying awareness week or month.

Exercise: Making a Movement Possible

How can you create the conditions that will best empower the kids in your school, community, or even family to take a leadership role in changing destructive social norms and bringing an end to bullying? Write down at least three concrete actions you can take to facilitate the process of a child being able to genuinely lead peers toward positive social change.

"You Are Asking Me to Stand Out on Purpose?"

An important consideration when it comes to empowering student-led initiatives is that many young people spend the majority of their waking hours trying not to stand apart from the crowd or to rock the boat in any way. Fitting in, in fact, is often a child's first line of defense against becoming a target of bullying. To have the confidence to stand out in a leadership role, kids must first believe that they will be safe in doing so.

As the old saying goes, there is safety in numbers. Student-led initiatives to stop bullying are an ideal vehicle for the activities of the buddy programs discussed in Key 6. When a student with high social capital partners with a more vulnerable one to develop and promote a grassroots antibullying campaign, the two can draw strength from one another initially and grow in their momentum as they inspire other students from all ends of the school's social hierarchy. While adults are wise to stay in the background of kids' initiatives and allow the student body to perceive the leadership as fully student driven, it is clear that professionals play a pivotal role in encouraging kid alliances, structuring successful projects, and supporting antibullying campaigns every step of the way.

Student-led initiatives can be as diverse as the young people themselves, but the following are several ideas for campaigns and small-group activities that kids can launch in their own schools and communities.

Petitions

In recent years, Web sites like Change.org have made it easy for even a single, dedicated individual to spark large-scale movements by making petitions available to mass audiences. No more walking door to door to gather signatures. Petitions can now reach the masses with just a few clicks of a mouse. Katy Butler was just 17 years old in 2012 when she launched a petition to change the R rating of the film *Bully* to a PG-13 rating so that the documentary could become accessible to mass young audiences. Her petition garnered more than half a million signatures. Within weeks, the MPAA did, indeed, change the film's rating and Katy became a role model for young people wanting to stand up to stop bullying.

Pledges

Pledges are another way that students have channeled their efforts toward getting large groups of people to commit to stopping bullying behaviors. One by one, as individuals sign specific pledges, entire schools and communities grow in their awareness of specific actions they can take to change destructive social norms and support positive ones. Effective pledges should be authored by the students who are initiating the campaign and include a list of specific desirable behaviors (e.g., "When I see bullying happening, I will do something about it. I will not just walk away or assume someone else will step in to stop it"). While pledges are certainly not legally binding, the gesture of signing one can be an important commitment of values by a student, and the mere act of creating a document that reaches dozens of peers is a powerful act of leadership by a young person.

T-Shirts

Blue is the customary color for bullying awareness. An easy-to-organize event for students is inviting everyone to wear a blue shirt on a designated day, as a show of support and solidarity for kids who have been bullied and as a commitment to stop bullying behaviors. This is the type of activity that channels young people's desire to fit in in a positive way. Blue ribbons can also be worn on backpacks or jackets as a daily sign of support for bullying prevention.

Bullying Awareness Walks

Picture a sea of bright blue T-shirts in a school hallway. Better yet, envision hundreds of kids, parents, and community members coming together on a walk, all clad in bullying awareness blue, to raise money—or just raise awareness—about the problem of bullying. Walks can be organized by kids for an entire community or simply for school students and staff: the sky is the limit with student-led initiatives, but at the same time, they don't have to be far flung in order to make a big impact. Two loops around the playground can be enough to alert the entire student body that bullying behaviors are not acceptable and that the whole school is making stopping bullying a priority.

Give Everyone a Place to Sit at the Table

As noted in the Key 1, bullying often takes place outside of the classroom, in undersupervised areas such as hallways, buses, locker rooms, and cafeterias. Adults can prompt students to focus their efforts on stopping bullying in these key areas. For example, students can work toward establishing seating arrangements in school cafeterias that ensure everyone has a friendly place to sit, every day.

Promote Kindness

Instead of campaigns that focus on all of the Thou Shalt Nots of bullying, student-led initiatives can promote building school cultures of respect by encouraging fun ways that kids can show kindness to each other. Public recognition of good works over the school's

PA system or student-led announcements highlighting random acts of kindness can be engaging ways of recognizing individuals for their positive behaviors. The trick in these sorts of initiatives is making sure that the students who would benefit from kindness the most do not end up left out in the cold, while students who already enjoy high social status shower each other with adoration. Adults play a key role in making sure that acts of kindness for some do not end up functioning as acts of exclusion for others.

Personal Power Circle
Bullying often makes kids feel powerless. The development of personal power circles can help kids regain feelings of control in the face of witnessing or being on the receiving end of bullying. Students interested in making a difference in stopping bullying can lead small groups of their peers in this simple but empowering, no-cost, three-step paper-and-pen activity:

1. First, kids should ask their peers to draw a medium-sized circle on the center of their page. Inside the circle, they should write down all of the things that they are not in control of when it comes to bullying (e.g., the actions of the bully, the location, the responses of their peers). Allow one minute for this activity.
2. Next, kids should instruct their peers to draw a large circle around the existing one. Inside of this circle, they should write down all of the things they do have control over when it comes to bullying. Students should encourage their peers to be creative and to think big about all of the things they can do to stop bullying (e.g., reach out to the child being bullied, refuse to laugh or feed into the bullying in any way, alert an adult, tell the child who is bullying to knock it off). Allow at least two minutes for this part of the activity.
3. Last, kids should lead a discussion among their peers acknowledging that when it comes to bullying, there are some things that kids can't control, but there are even more things that kids can do to take a powerful role in stopping bullying. The emphasis should be on students helping each other to know their own strength in

stopping bullying and to gain a sense of their own personal power in making a difference to change their worlds.

Adults can lead this type of activity as well, but the real power of it comes from kids inspiring each other toward taking action to stop bullying.

Eight-Word Memoirs

An activity that I frequently use when concluding any bullying presentation is to challenge participants to sum up what they have learned through a simple eight-word memoir. Kids can offer this challenge to their peers on a small-group or school-wide basis, challenging their classmates to phrase antibullying lessons in a pithy, easy-to-remember phrase. Eight-word memoirs can be drawn on poster board and put up on classroom walls or school hallways. They can be shared at school assemblies, printed on blue T-shirts, and published in annual yearbooks. The creation of eight-word memoirs is a simple activity that kids can lead on their own and a great way to get entire student bodies thinking about—and talking about—bringing an end to bullying.

My eight-word memoir, and a fitting end to this book:

Little things become big things in stopping bullying.

10 Practical Strategies to Keep the Conversation Going

1. Do not allow school or local politics to drive a denial of the existence of bullying. Conflict is a normal part of life; teaching kids how to cope with it is a part of education.
2. As a parent, be a tireless advocate for your child if he or she is being bullied.
3. As a school staff member, keep the subject of stopping bullying on the forefront of everyone's mind, throughout the school year (not just when a bullying crisis occurs).

4. Plan activities for kids, professionals, parents, and community members so that all interested parties are actively engaged in ending bullying.

5. Involve kids in antibullying initiatives to give them a sense of pride, ownership, and commitment to stopping bullying.

6. Survey students about their experiences and observations of bullying in your school.

7. Solicit ideas from students on how to turn their school's antibullying policies into daily practice.

8. Organize kids into small groups and challenge them to think about what can be done in their school, program, home, and community to change the culture of bullying.

9. Sponsor a school-wide contest in which kids design an antibullying T-shirt. Make the winning design a part of the school uniform for a day, week, month, or year.

10. Move beyond school reputations and personal insecurities in order to truly meet the needs of children.

Resources

With the Internet at all of our fingertips, information abounds, grassroots organizations grow, and helping organizations thrive. Indeed, the antibullying movement is an energized one, which is good news for all of us. Whittling down a universe of valuable resources into a manageable list of resources for readers is a daunting task. The following is not an exhaustive list of available books, organizations, and bullying-related Web sites, but rather a bite-sized one that is intended to give you direction without overwhelming your senses. Note that a separate list of social and emotional learning (SEL) resources, including recommended books for kids and activity-based programs for professionals and parents, is provided in Key 5.

Books

Bullied: What Every Parent, Teacher, and Kid Needs to Know About Ending the Cycle of Fear, by Carrie Goldman. With her own young child's experiences as a catalyst for her exploration of the issue of bullying, Goldman shares with readers effective strategies for helping kids cope with bullying and building communities of acceptance and respect.

Bully: An Action Plan for Teachers, Parents, and Communities to Combat the Bullying Crisis, by Lee Hirsch and Cynthia Lowen with Dina Santorelli. A companion to Hirsch's groundbreaking 2012 documentary film, *Bully*, this book is a compilation of articles, anecdotes, recommendations, and resources from antibullying experts, authors, and educators.

Bullying Hurts: Teaching Kindness Through Read Alouds and Guided Conversations, by Lester Laminack and Reba Wadsworth. This book is founded upon the authors' belief that read-aloud experiences and guided conversations can help adults bring an end to bullying. Laminack and Wadsworth show how selected children's literature can create community in the classroom and help educators meet Common Core State Standards at the same time.

Bullying in North American Schools, by Dorothy Espelage and Susan Swearer. This book provides a compilation of research on bullying among school-aged children, by leading experts in the field. It includes helpful suggestions for bullying prevention and intervention programs in schools and school districts.

Bullying Prevention and Intervention: Realistic Strategies for Schools, by Susan M. Swearer, Dorothy Espelage, and Scott Napolitano. The authors describe practical ways to stop bullying in schools. Step-by-step strategies are presented for school-based prevention and targeted intervention efforts. Special topics include how to involve teachers, parents, and peers in antibullying efforts.

Bullyproof Your Child for Life: Protect Your Child From Teasing, Taunting, and Bullying for Good, by Joel Haber and Jenna Glazer. This book offers specific strategies to help kids build resilience, develop compassion, and thrive in social dynamics. It applies to both boys and girls, from elementary through high school.

The Bully, the Bullied, and the Bystander: From Preschool to High School—How Parents and Teachers Can Help Break the Cycle of Violence, by Barbara Coloroso. Coloroso examines the three major players in most bullying situations and gives readers specific strategies for helping each one break the cycle of peer aggression. The updated version of this book contains a helpful section that addresses cyberbullying.

The Drama Years: Real Girls Talk About Surviving Middle School—Bullies, Brands, Body Image, and More, by Haley Kilpatrick and Whitney Joiner. Kilpatrick and Joiner offer a window into the worlds of middle school–aged girls, based on anecdotes from real girls around the country, giving readers insight into the drama of young friendships and the challenges of navigating conflict during these transitional years.

Girlfighting: Betrayal and Rejection Among Girls, by Lyn Mikel Brown. Through interviews of over 400 girls, author Lyn Mikel Brown examines how social norms nurture and reinforce meanness in girls. She asserts that pressure to hide angry feelings often results in girls expressing themselves through relational aggression and other non-direct communication.

Odd Girl Out: The Hidden Culture of Aggression in Girls, by Rachel Simmons. *Odd Girl Out* is a revealing look into the world of relational aggression. Using real-life stories, Simmons helps readers understand the underrated challenges facing young girls and provides important strategies for supporting kids through challenging years.

Queen Bees and Wannabes: Helping Your Daughter Survive Cliques, Gossip, Boyfriends, and the New Realities of Girl World, by Rosalind Wiseman. The book that inspired the Hollywood film *Mean Girls* and shone a bright light on the once-hidden nature of girls' friendships and conflict. Wiseman's keen insights into the world of tweens and teens is eye-opening for professionals and parents.

Reviving Ophelia: Saving the Selves of Adolescent Girls, by Mary Pipher. Pipher was one of the first authors to bring attention to the social pressures imposed on girls and to explore publicly how these pressures impact girls' behavior, from bullying to eating disorders, addictions, and mental health struggles.

School Climate 2.0: Preventing Cyberbullying and Sexting One Classroom at a Time, by Sameer Hinduja and Justin Patchin. Based on their extensive research through the Cyberbullying Research Center, Hinduja and Patchin connect kids' use of technology with the school environment and provide tools for creating a positive school climate that counteracts cyberbullying and sexting.

Sticks and Stones: Defeating the Culture of Bullying and Rediscovering the Power of Character and Empathy, by Emily Bazelon. Carefully researched and finely detailed, Bazelon's book explores the real-life experiences of three bullied young people, helping readers understand what 21st-century bullying is all about and how adults can help kids cope with it.

Web sites and Organizations

The Anti-Defamation League, originally founded to stop the defamation of Jewish people, now serves as one of the nation's premier civil rights and human relations agencies. Its **A World of Difference Institute** is a leader in developing antibullying training, curriculum, and resources for youth (www.adl.org).

The Bully Project is the social action campaign inspired by the award-winning documentary *Bully*. Their Web site features the Educators DVD Activation Toolkit, which includes information, activity ideas, discussion starters, and much more for continuing the movement to stop bullying (www.thebullyproject.com).

Collaborative for Academic, Social and Emotional Learning (CASEL), cofounded by renowned *Emotional Intelligence* author Daniel Goleman, is a not-for-profit organization that works to establish social and emotional learning as an essential part of education (www.casel.org).

Committee for Children is a nonprofit organization that works globally to promote children's social and academic success. Its comprehensive bullying prevention resources include the Steps to Respect and Second Step programs for elementary and middle school students (www.cfchildren.org).

The Cyberbullying Research Center, created by researchers Sameer Hinduja and Justin Patchin, provides provide up-to-date information about the nature and extent of online aggression among adolescents. It offers resources for educators, parents, and teens on understanding and stopping cyberbullying (www.cyberbullying.us).

Facing History and Ourselves is an organization that engages educators to teach civic responsibility, tolerance, and social action to young people. Its *A Guide to the Film BULLY: Fostering Empathy and Action in Schools* provides information about bullying, resources for creating safe and caring school environments, and a toolbox of discussion strategies to facilitate honest, open dialogue about the film (www.facinghistory.org).

The Gay, Lesbian, and Straight Education Network (GLSEN) is the leading national education organization focused on ensuring safe schools for all students. Its National School Climate Survey provides information on LGBT students who are bullied, harassed, or discriminated against to the Office of Civil Rights (www.glsen .org).

Kind Campaign is an internationally recognized movement, documentary, and school program created by Lauren Parsekian and Molly Thompson, two college friends affected by female bullying who aim to bring awareness and healing to the impact of relational aggression (www.kindcampaign.com).

The Megan Meier Foundation was established by Tina Meier in honor of her daughter Megan, who committed suicide at the age of 13 after relentless cyberbullying victimization. The foundation's mission is to make a difference by spreading Megan's story and teaching

Internet safety to kids until bullying and cyberbullying are nonexistent (www.meganmeierfoundation.org).

National Center for Learning Disabilities (NCLD) aims to improve the lives of all people with learning difficulties and disabilities through empowerment and advocacy activities. The NCLD has partnered with the Bully Project to draw attention to the nationwide problem of bullying and to commit time and resources to prevent and stop bullying (www.ncld.org).

National School Climate Center (NCSS) is an organization that helps schools integrate social and emotional learning with academic instruction. NSCC partners with schools to prevent bullying and promote upstander behaviors in various ways. Important resources include their Breaking the Bully-Victim-Bystander Cycle Tool Kit: Creating a Climate of Safety and Social Responsibility (www.school climate.org).

The Olweus Bullying Prevention Program (OBPP), originally founded in Norway, is among the most widely used bullying prevention programs in the world. Its system-wide approach addresses change on four distinct levels: the individual, the classroom, the school, and the community. (www.violencepreventionworks.org)

PACER's National Bullying Prevention Center provides resources designed to benefit all students, including those with disabilities. Its goal is to unite, engage, and educate communities nationwide to prevent bullying through creative, relevant, and interactive resources (www.PACERkidsagainstbullying.org and www.PACER TeensAgainstBullying.org).

ParentCentral.net is the sister site to TeenCentral, providing a place where parents can communicate with counselors and other parenting professionals and receive answers within 24 hours (www .parentcentral.net).

Roots of Empathy is an evidence-based classroom program that has shown significant results in reducing aggression among school children while raising social and emotional competence and increasing empathy. Its unique approach features an infant and parent who visit a school classroom every three weeks over the school year. Through interactions with the parent and child, young learners become more competent in understanding their own feelings and the feelings of others (empathy) and less likely to bully each other (www .rootsofempathy.org).

Stand for the Silent is the platform through which Kirk and Laura Smalley share the story of their son, Ty Field-Smalley, the 11-year-old boy featured in *Bully*, who committed suicide after being suspended from school for retaliating against a bully that had been bullying him for over two years. Stand for the Silent offers education and tools aimed at preventing the Smalleys' tragedy from happening to another child and family (www.standforthesilent.com).

Stop-Bullies.com provides professionals and parents with relevant and up-to-date bully prevention information through their monthly e-newsletter, presentations, trainings, and consultations (www.stop-bullies.com).

StopBullying.gov, a Web site managed by the U.S. Department of Health and Human Services, offers information, updates, and resources about bullying to parents, professionals, community members, and kids (www.stopbullying.gov).

Stop Bullying Now is a Web site featuring the research and findings of Stan Davis, who, along with Dr. Charisse Nixon, pioneered the Youth Voice Research Project. Stop Bullying Now features strategies, advice, research, and interventions for ending bullying (www.stopbullyingnow.com).

Stop Bullying: Speak Up, offered by the Cartoon Network, uses celebrities, videos, a Stop Bullying pledge, and other kid-appealing messages to reach young people with their strong antibullying message. Stop Bullying: Speak Up also offers tips, strategies, and a complete toolkit for parents and educators (http://www.cartoonnetwork.com/promos/stopbullying/index.html).

STOP Cyberbullying is a program created by lawyer and cyberbullying expert Parry Aftab and the Wired Safety Group. The Web site provides information, tips, a Stop Cyberbullying Toolkit, and the Alex Wonder Kid Cyberdetective Agency game to help stop cyberbullying (www.stopcyberbullying.org).

Sweethearts and Heroes is the organization established by Tom Murphy and Jason Spector, two dynamic presenters who use their background as Mixed Martial Arts (MMA) competitors to engage students and give them an important message about tolerance, bullying awareness, and most importantly an action plan of what to do when bullying happens. It is Tom and Jason's collective goal to help foster a school climate where kids refuse to let bullying happen (www.sweetheartsandheroes.com).

TeenCentral.net is a completely free and anonymous site that young people can visit to share their personal stories, read about the experiences of their peers, and offer support to fellow users. Different from a chat room or message board, however, feedback is monitored by professional counselors who also provide expert responses to youth stories. TeenCentral features resources specifically for helping kids understand and cope with bullying (www.teencentral.net).

The Trevor Project is the leading national organization providing crisis intervention and suicide prevention services to LGBTQ youth. In addition to operating the only national crisis lifeline for LGBTQ teens and young adults, Trevor has been a leading crisis resource for antibullying initiatives (www.trevorproject.org).

The Youth Voice Project is the work of Stan Davis and Dr. Charisse Nixon. Its goal is to compile a body of knowledge describing the most helpful interventions to reduce bullying and harassment in schools. Davis and Nixon aim to use this information to guide educators, parents, and youth in applying effective interventions to reduce bullying and optimize students' development (www.youth voiceproject.com).

References

Anthony, M., & Lindert, R. (2010). *Little girls can be mean: Four steps to bully-proof girls in the early grades.* New York: St. Martin's Griffen.

Bazelon, E. (2013). *Sticks and stones: Defeating the culture of bullying and rediscovering the power of character and empathy.* New York: Random House.

Borba, M. (2009). *The big book of parenting solutions: 101 answers to your everyday challenges and wildest worries.* San Francisco: Jossey-Bass.

Brokenleg, M., & Long, N. (2013). Problems as opportunity: Meeting growth needs. *Reclaiming Children and Youth, 22*(1), 36–37.

Brown, P. L. (2013, April 3). Opening up, students transform a vicious circle. *New York Times.* Retrieved from http://www.nytimes.com/2013/04/04/education/restorative-justice-programs-take-root-in-schools.html?pagewanted=all&_r=0

Centre for Justice and Reconciliation. (2008). What is restorative justice? [Briefing paper]. Retrieved from http://www.pfi.org/cjr/restorative-justice/introduction-to-restorative-justice-practice-and-outcomes/briefings/what-is-restorative-justice

Center for Safe Schools. (2012). *Pennsylvania Bullying Prevention Toolkit: Resources for parents, educators, and professionals serving children, youth and families.* Retrieved from http://www.safeschools.info/bp_toolkit.pdf

Centers for Disease Control and Prevention. (2012). Prevalence of autism spectrum disorders—Autism and Developmental Disabilities Monitoring Network, 14 sites, United States, 2008. *MMWR, 61*(SS03), 1–19. Retrieved from http://www.cdc.gov/mmwr/preview/mmwrhtml/ss6103a1.htm?s_cid=ss6103a1_

Chambers, J. C. (2012, June 24). Kid whispering tactics: The inside kid. Lecture at Black Hills Seminars, Reclaiming Youth Conference, Rapid City, SD.

Collaborative for Academic, Social, and Emotional Learning (CASEL).

(2011). Bullying: Social and emotional learning and bullying prevention. Retrieved from http://casel.org/in-schools/bullying/

Collier, A., Swearer, S., Doces, M., & Jones, L. (2012). *Changing the culture: Ideas for student action.* Retrieved from the Born This Way Foundation and the Berkman Center for Internet and Society at Harvard University:http://cyber.law.harvard.edu/sites/cyber.law.harvard.edu/files/IdeasForStudents.pdf

Coloroso, B. (2008). *The bully, the bullied, and the bystander: From preschool to high school—how parents and teachers can help break the cycle of violence.* New York: HarperCollins.

Committee for Children. (2013). Social-emotional learning and bullying prevention [white paper]. Retrieved from http://www.cfchildren.org/Portals/0/Home/H_DOC/SEL_Bullying_Paper.pdf

Crouch, G. (2013). Issue SnapShot: Cyber-bullying. Retrieved from MediaBadger: http://www.scribd.com/doc/151972890/SocMed-Snap-Bullying-Jun13-CH

Davis, S., & Nixon, C. (2010). *The Youth Voice Research Project: Victimization and strategies.* Retrieved from http://www.youthvoiceproject.com/

Dewar, G. (2008). When bullies get bullied by others: Understanding bully-victims. Retrieved from Parenting Science: http://www.parentingscience.com/bully-victims.html

DiMarco, J. (2011, October 28). Parents take the lead to prevent bullying [blog post]. *Parenting.* Retrieved from http://www.parenting.com/blogs/mom-congress/jacqui-dimarco/parents-take-lead-prevent-bullying

Eliot, M., & Cornell, D. (2009). Bullying in middle school as a function of insecure attachment and aggressive attitudes. *School Psychology International, 30*(2), 201–214. http://dx.doi.org/10.1177/0143034309104148

Ericson, N. (2001). *Addressing the problem of juvenile bullying.* FS-200127. Washington, DC: U.S. Department of Justice, Office of Justice Programs, Office of Juvenile Justice and Delinquency Programs.

Espelage, D. L., & Swearer, S. M. (Eds.). (2010). *Bullying in North American schools.* New York: Routledge.

Faris, R., & Felmlee, D. (2011). Status struggles: Network centrality and gender segregation in same- and cross-gender aggression. *American Sociological Review, 76,* 48–73.

Goldman, C. (2012). *Bullied: What every parent, teacher, and kid needs to know about ending the cycle of fear.* New York: Harper One.

Haber, J. (2007). *Bullyproof your child for life.* New York: Perigee Trade.

Harvard Graduate School of Education. (2013). Assess the school environment. Retrieved from http://isites.harvard.edu/icb/icb.do?keyword =making_caring_common&pageid=icb.page575161

Hawkins, D. L., Pepler, D. J., & Craig, W. M. (2001). Naturalistic observations of peer interventions in bullying. *Social Development, 10*(4), 512–527.

Hinduja, S., & Patchin, J. (2010). Cyberbullying: Identification, prevention and response [fact sheet]. Retrieved from http://www.cyber bullying.us/cyberbullying_fact_sheet.pdf

Hirsch, L., & Lowen, C. (Eds.). (2012). *Bully: An action plan for teachers, parents, and communities to combat the bullying crisis.* New York: Weinstein.

Horowitz, S. H. (2013). The truth about bullying and LD. Retrieved from National Center for Learning Disabilities: http://www.ncld .org/parents-child-disabilities/bullying/truth-about-bullying-ld

Kraft, E. M., & Wang, J. (2009, July–December). Effectiveness of cyber bullying prevention strategies: A study on students' perspectives. *International Journal of Cyber Criminology, 3,* 513–535. Retrieved from www.cybercrimejournal.com/KraftwangJulyIJCC2009.pdf

Laugeson, L. (2013). Comebacks for being teased [video file]. Retrieved from Kidsinthehouse: http://www.kidsinthehouse.com/video/come backs-being-teased

Long, N., Long, J., & Whitson, S. (2009). *The angry smile: The psychology of passive aggressive behavior in families, schools, and workplaces* (2nd ed.). Austin, TX: Pro-ED.

Ludwig, T. (2010). *Confessions of a former bully.* New York: Random House.

Ludwig, T. (2013, February 20). How to talk to your kids about bullying [blog post]. Retrieved from http://www.aplatformforgood.org/blog/ entry/how-to-talk-to-your-kids-about-bullying

Lumeng, J. C., Forrest, P., Appugliese, D. P., Kaciroti, N., Corwyn, R. F., & Bradley, R. H. (2010). Weight status as a predictor of being bullied in third through sixth grades. *Pediatrics, 125*(6), e1301–e1307. http://dx.doi: 10.1542/peds.2009-0774

Marini, Z., & Dane, A. (2010). What's a bully-victim? Retrieved from Education.com: http://www.education.com/reference/article/what-is-a-bully-victim/

McCready, A. (2012). A little "I'm sorry" goes a long way. In L. Hirsch & C. Lowen (Eds.), *Bully: An action plan for teachers, parents, and communities to combat the bullying crisis* (pp. 71–87). New York: Weinstein.

Olweus, D., Limber, S. P., Flerx, V. C., Mullin, N., Riese, J., & Snyder, M. (2007). *Olweus bullying prevention program: Teacher guide.* Center City, MN: Hazelden.

PACER's National Bullying Prevention Center. (2012). Statistics on Bullying. Retrieved from http://www.pacer.org/bullying/about/media-kit/stats.asp.

Rodkin, P. C., & Hodges, E. V. E. (2003). Bullies and victims in the peer ecology: Four questions for psychologists and school professionals. *School Psychology Review, 32*(3), 384–400. Retrieved from http://courses.washington.edu/nurs509/bully/PeerEcology.pdf

Savage, D. (2012). *It gets better: Coming out, overcoming bullying, and creating a life worth living.* New York: Plume

Schumacher, A. W. (2013, February 19). "Bully" is not a noun [blog post]. Retrieved from Committee for Children: http://www.cfchildren.org/advocacy/about-us/e-newsletter/articletype/articleview/articleid/16593.aspx

Silverman, R. (2012). Bullying has legs . . . and teeth. In L. Hirsch & C. Lowen (Eds.), *Bully: An action plan for teachers, parents, and communities to combat the bullying crisis* (pp. 47–59). New York: Weinstein.

Simmons, R. (2010). *The curse of the good girl: Raising authentic girls with courage and confidence.* New York: Penguin.

Simmons, R. (2011). *Odd girl out: The hidden culture of aggression in girls.* New York: First Mariner.

Sourander, A., Jensen, P., Rönning, J. A., Niemelä, S., Helenius, H., Sillanmäki, L . . . Almqvist, F. (2007). What is the early adulthood outcome of boys who bully or are bullied in childhood? The Finnish "From a Boy to a Man" study. *Pediatrics, 120*(2), 397–404. Retrieved from http://www.pediatricsdigest.mobi/content/120/2/397.full

Stanford University Medical Center. (2007, April 12). School bullying affects majority of elementary students. *ScienceDaily.* Retrieved October 21, 2013, from http://www.sciencedaily.com/releases/2007/04/070412072345.htm

Steinberg, L. (2008). A social neuroscience perspective on adolescent risk-taking. *Developmental Review, 28,* 78–106.

Taylor, R. (Producer). (2013, June 25). Sweethearts and heroes: A STT exclusive [audio podcast]. Retrieved from Spreaker: http://www.spreaker.com/user/smarterteamtraining/sweethearts_and_heroes_a_stt_exclusive

Tucker, C. J., Finkelhor, D., Turner, H., & Shattuck, A. (2013). Association of sibling aggression with child and adolescent mental health. *Pediatrics, 132*(1), 79–84; published ahead of print June 17, 2013, doi:10.1542/peds.2012-3801.

U.S. Department of Health and Human Services. (2013). Bullying and children and youth with disabilities and special health needs. Retrieved from http://www.stopbullying.gov/at-risk/groups/special-needs/BullyingTipSheet.pdf

Wendorf, J. (2012). Bullying's special problem. In L. Hirsch & C. Lowen (Eds.), *Bully: An action plan for teachers, parents, and communities to combat the bullying crisis* (pp. 105–108). New York: Weinstein.

Whitson, S. (2011a). *Friendship and other weapons: Group activities to help young girls aged 5–11 to cope with bullying.* London: Jessica Kingsley.

Whitson, S. (2011b). *How to be angry: An assertive anger expression group guide for kids and teens.* London: Jessica Kingsley.

Willick, F. (2013, July 5). Cyberbullies branch out. *Chronicle Herald.* Retrieved from http://thechronicleherald.ca/novascotia/1140177-cyberbullies-branch-out#.UdlGlDo9gns.facebook

Wilton, M. M., Craig, W. M., & Pepler, D. J. (2000). Emotional regulation and display in classroom victims of bullying: Characteristic expressions of affect, coping styles, and relevant contextual factors. *Social Development, 9*(2), 226–245.

Winner, M. G. (2013, May 9). Implementing Social Thinking® concepts and vocabulary into the home and school day. *Social Thinking.* Lecture conducted in Hunt Valley, MD.

Wiseman, R. (2009). *Queen bees and wannabees: Helping your daughter survive cliques, gossip, boyfriends, and the new realities of girl world.* New York: Three Rivers.

Wright, J. (2013, April 19). *Bullying: What it is and what schools can do about it.* Retrieved from Intervention Central: http://www.interventioncentral.org/behavioral-interventions/bully-prevention/bullying-what-it-what-schools-can-do-about-it

Index